T0340169

The Cambridge Introduction to
Franz Kafka

Franz Kafka (1883–1924) is one of the most influential of modern authors, whose darkly fascinating novels and stories – where themes such as power, punishment and alienation loom large – have become emblematic of modern life. This *Introduction* offers a clear and accessible account of Kafka's life, work and literary influence and overturns many myths surrounding them. His texts are in fact far more engaging, diverse, light-hearted and ironic than is commonly suggested by clichés of 'the Kafkaesque'. And, once explored in detail, they are less difficult and impenetrable than is often assumed. Through close analysis of their style, imagery and narrative perspective, Carolin Duttlinger aims to give readers the confidence to (re-)discover Kafka's works without constant recourse to the mantras of critical orthodoxy. In addition, she situates Kafka's texts within their wider cultural, historical and political contexts, illustrating how they respond to the concerns of their age, and of our own.

CAROLIN DUTTLINGER is University Lecturer in German at the University of Oxford, Ockenden Fellow in German at Wadham College, Oxford, and Co-Director of the Oxford Kafka Research Centre. She is the author of *Kafka and Photography* (2007) and the editor, with Ben Morgan and Anthony Phelan, of *Walter Benjamins anthropologisches Denken* (2012).

The Cambridge Introduction to
Franz Kafka

CAROLIN DUTTLINGER

 CAMBRIDGE
UNIVERSITY PRESS

CAMBRIDGE
UNIVERSITY PRESS

University Printing House, Cambridge CB2 8BS, United Kingdom

Cambridge University Press is part of the University of Cambridge.

It furthers the University's mission by disseminating knowledge in the pursuit of
education, learning and research at the highest international levels of excellence.

www.cambridge.org
Information on this title: www.cambridge.org/9780521757713

First published 2013

A catalogue record for this publication is available from the British Library

Library of Congress Cataloguing in Publication data
Duttlinger, Carolin, 1976–
The Cambridge introduction to Franz Kafka / Carolin Duttlinger.
    pages   cm
Includes bibliographical references and index.
ISBN 978-0-521-75771-3
1. Kafka, Franz, 1883–1924 – Criticism and interpretation.   I. Title.
PT2621.A26Z6783   2013
833'.912–dc23

                                                      2012044015

ISBN 978-0-521-76038-6 Hardback
ISBN 978-0-521-75771-3 Paperback

For Joe, Max and Clara

Contents

4 Scholarship and adaptations

Illustrations

Preface

Kafka is one of the most iconic of modern writers and probably the most widely read German-language author of all times. A century on, his works have lost none of their strangeness and appeal; while the 'Kafka industry' continues to produce books and articles at a dizzying rate, Kafka's influence is by no means limited to the ivory towers of academia. Indeed, he is one of the few authors whose fame straddles the boundary between high and popular culture. Yet Kafka's enduring and almost universal popularity is something of a mixed blessing, since for many this might make him appear offputtingly trendy in a shallow, vaguely postmodern way. Surely an author whose works have appealed to so many cannot have real substance? Even if we are not deterred by Kafka's fame, we cannot avoid the questions it poses. (Is Kafka perhaps too famous for his own good, too famous to be read seriously?) Arguably, we know both too much and too little about Kafka. The myth of Kafka the isolated, otherworldly genius seems to resist all evidence to the contrary, and his problematic relationship with his father – admittedly documented by Kafka himself – is often applied to his texts as a one-size-fits-all interpretative template. But Kafka has also often been cited as the Existentialist, nihilist, Zionist or Freudian writer par excellence, or as a kind of prophet who predicted the Holocaust. The dilemma surrounding Kafka's fame is encapsulated by the term 'Kafkaesque'. In contrast to similar coinages, such as 'Shakespearean', 'Proustian' or 'Wildean', 'Kafkaesque' is used not only as an adjective but also as a noun. 'The Kafkaesque' is a term not limited to literary contexts but which has become a shorthand for a wide range of artistic techniques, situations and experiences. The *Oxford English Dictionary* defines it as 'Of or relating to the writings of Franz Kafka; resembling the state of affairs or a state of mind described by Kafka'. This appropriately vague, tautological definition leaves it open to which aspect of Kafka's writings the term refers, and indeed 'Kafkaesque' can be used in different, even incompatible, ways. It can refer to Kafka's strange and darkly comical storylines (a man's never-explained transformation into an insect, another man's equally mysterious arrest by a faceless institution), to the more general absurd and oppressive mood pervading his texts, or to particular narrative techniques which defy the reader's expectations and resist conclusive interpretation.

So the notion of the Kafkaesque is sufficiently vague to make it ubiquitous, but this ubiquity leads to another problem. It implies that there is something recognizable and distinctive, even unique, about Kafka's texts, but at the same time suggests that this quality is not limited to Kafka's texts but can be transferred, emulated or indeed parodied. What is more, as my examples of Kafka's darkly comical plotlines above suggest, the term in its core meaning is probably derived from just two texts: *The Metamorphosis* and *The Trial*. Although these two works – undoubtedly Kafka's most famous – seem to form a neat diptych of Kafka's universe, involving brutal fathers, transgressive desires and labyrinthine, faceless institutions, *The Metamorphosis* and *The Trial* are also problematic showcases. As we will see in more detail later, Kafka did not like the ending of the former, and went about writing the latter in an atypical, experimental way. Ultimately, he was unhappy with both texts. So if *The Trial* and *The Metamorphosis* have become emblematic of his writings more generally, this is at the expense of his lesser-known works, at the expense of a more diverse and comprehensive picture.

The purpose of this book is to provide such a picture, by returning to Kafka's texts with careful close readings that bring out their inner tensions and complexities. For this purpose, I will put particular emphasis on Kafka's rhetoric and style – on the meandering, often contradictory or paradoxical ways in which his plots unfold, and on the grammatical intricacies of his texts. To read Kafka well, to appreciate why he his – rightly – one of the most famous of modern writers, is to read him slowly and in close detail, rather than to just look out for the big 'headline' issues of guilt and power, punishment and alienation. This is one main challenge of reading Kafka; another concerns our understanding of what Kafka's work *is*. For readers wanting to gain a first insight into his writings, editions of his three novels and of the short stories are the natural starting point, but even here we run into problems. For the vast majority of Kafka's writings, including the novels and many short stories, remained unfinished, work in progress. To read these texts as self-contained, coherent works is to distort and misunderstand the fluid nature of Kafka's texts, many of which emerged out of an amorphous (and often intermittent) writing stream, which was channelled into self-contained pieces only retrospectively, by either Kafka himself or his editors.

One of my aims in this Introduction is to draw attention to the fluid and provisional nature of Kafka's texts by focusing on what could be described as the 'margins' of these writings: deletions, corrections, alternative formulations, fragments and discarded drafts, the vast majority of which have not been translated into English. In addition, I will juxtapose famous and less famous texts. The result should be a more interesting Kafka, an author who is worth reading time and again, in detail and beyond the narrow scope of his most famous works. I hope this will provide readers with the tools and the incentive to explore those texts which, for reasons of space, I have been unable to discuss. These include, among Kafka's longer pieces, 'The Huntsman Gracchus', 'Blumfeld, an Elderly Bachelor' and 'The Village Schoolmaster', as well as the Zürau aphorisms and many other texts and fragments.

Acknowledgements

My research for this study was made possible by the Zvi Meitar/Vice-Chancellor Oxford University Research Prize. I am also grateful to Wadham College, Oxford, and the Faculty of Medieval and Modern Languages at the University of Oxford for their generous support of the project. My own ideas on Kafka have been shaped by conversations with colleagues and students too numerous to mention. I am particularly indebted to Ritchie Robertson and Joe Harris for their meticulous proofreading skills, to Dora Osborne for providing invaluable help with the translation of quotations, and to Linda Bree and everyone else at Cambridge University Press for their constructive feedback and support.

Abbreviations

The abbreviations used in this book are listed below. Where a published translation is available, all quotations are referenced first to the English version and then to the German original, in each case followed by a page number. On occasion, translations have been tacitly modified from the published versions; for those works which have not been translated I have given my own translations.

Fictional writings

C   *The Castle*, trans. Anthea Bell (Oxford: Oxford University Press, 2009)
CSS   *The Complete Stories*, ed. Nahum N. Glatzer (New York: Schocken, 1976)
DL   *Drucke zu Lebzeiten*, ed. Wolf Kittler, Hans-Gerd Koch and Gerhard Neumann. Franz Kafka: Schriften, Tagebücher, Briefe: Kritische Ausgabe (Frankfurt/Main: Fischer, 1996)
DLA   *Drucke zu Lebzeiten: Apparatband*, ed. Wolf Kittler, Hans-Gerd Koch and Gerhard Neumann. Franz Kafka: Schriften, Tagebücher, Briefe: Kritische Ausgabe (Frankfurt/Main: Fischer, 1996)
HA   *A Hunger Artist and Other Stories*, trans. Joyce Crick (Oxford: Oxford University Press, 2012)
M   *The Metamorphosis and Other Stories*, trans. Joyce Crick (Oxford: Oxford University Press, 2009)
MD   *The Man who Disappeared (America)*, trans. Ritchie Robertson (Oxford: Oxford University Press, 2012)
NS I   *Nachgelassene Schriften und Fragmente I*, ed. Malcolm Pasley. Franz Kafka: Schriften, Tagebücher, Briefe: Kritische Ausgabe (Frankfurt/Main: Fischer, 1993)
NS II   *Nachgelassene Schriften und Fragmente II*, ed. Malcolm Pasley. Franz Kafka: Schriften, Tagebücher, Briefe: Kritische Ausgabe (Frankfurt/Main: Fischer, 1992)

ON   *The Blue Octavo Notebooks*, ed. Max Brod, trans. Ernst Kaiser and
      Eithne Wilkins (Cambridge, MA: Exact Change, 1991)
P   *Der Proceß*, ed. Malcolm Pasley. Franz Kafka: Schriften, Tagebücher,
      Briefe: Kritische Ausgabe (Frankfurt/Main: Fischer, 1990)
PA   *Der Proceß: Apparatband*, ed. Malcolm Pasley. Franz Kafka:
      Schriften, Tagebücher, Briefe: Kritische Ausgabe (Frankfurt/Main:
      Fischer, 1990)
S   *Das Schloß*, ed. Malcolm Pasley. Franz Kafka: Schriften, Tagebücher,
      Briefe: Kritische Ausgabe (Frankfurt/Main: Fischer, 1982)
SA   *Das Schloß: Apparatband*, ed. Malcolm Pasley. Franz Kafka:
      Schriften, Tagebücher, Briefe: Kritische Ausgabe (Frankfurt/Main:
      Fischer, 1982)
T   *The Trial*, trans. Mike Mitchell (Oxford: Oxford University Press, 2009)
V   *Der Verschollene*, ed. Jost Schillemeit. Franz Kafka: Schriften,
      Tagebücher, Briefe: Kritische Ausgabe (Frankfurt/Main: Fischer, 1983)

Non-fictional writings

A   *Amtliche Schrifte*, ed. Klaus Hermsdorf and Benno Wagner. Franz
      Kafka: Schriften, Tagebücher, Briefe: Kritische Ausgabe (Frankfurt/
      Main: Fischer, 2004)
B   *Briefe 1902–1924*, ed. Max Brod (Frankfurt/Main: Fischer, 1975)
B1   *Briefe 1900–1912*, ed. Hans-Gerd Koch. Franz Kafka: Schriften,
      Tagebücher, Briefe: Kritische Ausgabe (Frankfurt/Main: Fischer, 1999)
B2   *Briefe 1913 – März 1914*, ed. Hans-Gerd Koch. Franz Kafka: Schriften,
      Tagebücher, Briefe: Kritische Ausgabe (Frankfurt/Main: Fischer,
      2001)
B3   *Briefe April 1914 – 1917*, ed. Hans-Gerd Koch. Franz Kafka: Schriften,
      Tagebücher, Briefe: Kritische Ausgabe (Frankfurt/Main: Fischer, 2005)
BE   *Briefe an die Eltern aus den Jahren 1922–1924*, ed. Josef Čermák and
      Martin Svatoš (Frankfurt/Main: Fischer, 1993)
BF   *Briefe an Felice und andere Korrespondenz aus der Verlobungszeit*, ed.
      Erich Heller and Jürgen Born (Frankfurt/Main: Fischer, 1998)
BM   *Briefe an Milena*, ed. Jürgen Born and Michael Müller, extended and
      revised edn (Frankfurt/Main: Fischer, 1999)
D   *The Diaries of Franz Kafka, 1910–23*, ed. Max Brod (London:
      Minerva, 1992)
LF   *Letters to Felice*, ed. Erich Heller and Jürgen Born, trans. James Stern
      and Elisabeth Duckworth (London: Minerva, 1992)

LFFE	*Letters to Friends, Family and Editors*, trans. Richard Winston and Clara Winston (Richmond: Oneworld Classics Ltd, 2011)
LM	*Letters to Milena*, ed. Willy Haas, trans. Tania and James Stern (London: Minerva, 1992)
O	*The Office Writings*, ed. Stanley Corngold, Jack Greenberg and Benno Wagner, trans. Eric Patton with Ruth Hein (Princeton: Princeton University Press, 2008)
TB	*Tagebücher*, ed. Hans-Gerd Koch, Michael Müller and Malcolm Pasley. Franz Kafka: Schriften, Tagebücher, Briefe: Kritische Ausgabe (Frankfurt/Main: Fischer, 1990)

Chapter 1

Life

Recent years have seen the publication of two illuminating Kafka biographies. Both Peter-André Alt and Reiner Stach defy the cliché of Kafka as an unrecognized genius whose works bore little connection to his age.[1] Although Kafka's life was externally uneventful, it was shaped, at decisive points, by the political events of his time, which left traces in his writings, and he was a close observer of cultural developments and debates. What is more, Kafka was far from isolated. In Prague he was part of a tight-knit group of writers and intellectuals, and he was also well travelled. While only a fraction of his work was published during his lifetime, and he was certainly no bestselling author, Kafka was held in high esteem by leading writers and publishers of his day.

1883–1912: childhood, youth and first employment

Franz Kafka was born in Prague on 3 July 1883 as the oldest child of Hermann Kafka (1852–1931) and his wife, Julie, née Löwy (1856–1934). Hermann was the son of a Jewish butcher; one of six children, he grew up in great poverty in a small south Bohemian village. Julie's parents, in contrast, were well-off, and counted doctors, merchants and Talmudic scholars among their ancestors. Kafka's parents were very different in terms of their social background and character, but both were hardworking and ambitious. They had moved to Prague in the 1870s, and their economic success enabled them to have a comfortable lifestyle. Like many Jews of their generation, they were assimilated into mainstream society, adopting its liberal bourgeois values, which in turn distanced them from their religious roots and traditions.

Following Franz's birth in 1883, the Kafkas had two further sons, Georg and Heinrich, who both died in infancy (in 1886 and 1888); their deaths must have cast a shadow over Franz's early childhood. The Kafkas then had three daughters: Gabriele ('Elli', 1889–1942), Valerie ('Valli', 1890–1942) and Ottilie ('Ottla', 1892–1943), to whom Kafka was later particularly close. Hermann Kafka ran a haberdashery shop in central Prague. He was a successful but dominant businessman, whose choleric disposition affected his relations with his employees and his family. Franz, a quiet, sensitive child, found his father's temper hard to stomach. Materially, Franz had a comfortable childhood, but since his mother was busy helping his father in the shop, he was looked after mostly by a succession of nannies and later a French-speaking governess. Between 1895 and 1907 the family moved seven times, reflecting their growing prosperity.

The Kafkas brought their children up to speak German, the language of the aspirational Jewish middle classes. At school, Kafka was also taught French, Czech, Latin and Greek. In 1901, he matriculated at the Charles University in Prague to study chemistry. After just two weeks, he switched to law, a move no doubt intended to please his parents, but this subject did not really chime with his interests either. In the following semester, Kafka attended lectures on German literature and art history, and even considered studying literature in Munich. In the end, he unenthusiastically continued with his law degree, looking for intellectual stimulation outside his studies. At the talks, debates and readings arranged by the German student organisation he got to know his lifelong friend Max Brod, a fellow law student and budding writer. Brod introduced him to the blind writer Oskar Baum and the philosophy student Felix Weltsch; together they formed a reading group, the nucleus of what Brod would later call the 'Prague circle'. Between 1909 and 1911, Kafka went on journeys, mostly with Brod, which took him to Switzerland, Italy and Paris, to Weimar, Leipzig and Berlin.

Having struggled through his law exams, Kafka was awarded the doctorate in law with the lowest pass mark in 1906. His first post, after a year of gaining professional experience in the Prague courts, was with the Prague branch of a Trieste-based insurance company. Frustrated with the long hours and menial pay, however, Kafka moved to the state-run Workers' Accident Insurance Institute for the Kingdom of Bohemia in 1908, where he would remain until his early retirement in 1922. In his new role he processed insurance claims and was involved in accident prevention by inspecting working conditions on-site. Among the main attractions of the new post were its hours. Kafka had to work from only 8 am to 2 pm, leaving him time to pursue his literary ambitions, although he still regarded his insurance post as a great distraction from writing. His at times humorous, at times desperate complaints about his day job are a recurring theme in his letters and diaries – and yet Kafka was a dedicated and able employee. The articles and reports he wrote for the Institute show his stylistic flair, as well as his expert knowledge and passionate commitment to workers' safety. Indeed, Kafka was greatly valued by both the Austrian and the subsequent Czech directorship. He started off in a modest position but quickly rose through the ranks and was treated with respect and generosity by his superiors, particularly during his later illness.

1912–1917: breakthrough, intimacy and crisis

By 1912, Kafka's professional career was well established. He still lived with his parents, as was customary for unmarried sons and daughters at the time, and although he had indulged in a few romantic dalliances and the occasional brothel visit – a common pastime for young men of his class – he had not been in a serious relationship. Encouraged by Brod, Kafka kept a diary, which was meant to give him regular writing practice, as well as fuel for his literary imagination. He had written two novel fragments and had published a few short stories in newspapers and magazines. Upon Brod's introduction, Kafka met the Leipzig-based publisher Kurt Wolff, who agreed to publish a volume of his short stories, *Meditation*. In August 1912, while putting the finishing touches to *Meditation*, Kafka met Felice Bauer, a successful career woman from Berlin, who worked in a firm making office equipment. It took Kafka over a month to write to Felice, but once the correspondence was underway, it quickly became more intimate. Kafka and Felice exchanged hundreds of letters, though only Kafka's side of the correspondence has survived. During the five years of their relationship, they met infrequently and, given Kafka's work commitments, often for just a few hours, although in 1916 they spent a few precious days alone together in the spa town of Marienbad.

Kafka's initial elation soon gave way to growing doubt – doubt about Felice's ability to understand his literary vocation, but also about his own suitability for married life. In tortured, self-accusing letters he tried to convince her that he would not make a suitable husband. In one famous letter he outlines his ideal mode of existence, which would be to sit 'in the innermost room of a spacious locked cellar with my writing things and a lamp' (14–15 January 1913; *LF* 156/*B2* 40); only in such complete isolation, he believed, would he be able to realize his creative potential. Initially, Felice was undeterred by Kafka's self-imposed asceticism, and in May 1914 they got engaged in Berlin; only two months later, however, she dissolved the engagement. A few months later Kafka and Felice resumed contact, and in August 1917 they renewed their engagement (see Fig. 1).

1 Kafka and Felice Bauer in Budapest (July 1917)

Shortly afterwards Kafka was diagnosed with tuberculosis and ended the engagement for good.

The relationship with Felice was Kafka's most difficult, but also his most formative, in both personal and creative terms. The day after he sent off his first letter to Berlin, he wrote the short story 'The Judgement', his literary breakthrough. In the five years between 1912 and 1917, Kafka produced two novels, as well as some of his most famous short stories. A close comparison between these prose works and Kafka's letters reveals many cross-connections; the extensive correspondence with Felice, which shared the same nocturnal space as his creative writing, was a source of inspiration and a space for self-reflection.

When the First World War broke out in August 1914, Kafka wrote in his diary, 'Germany has declared war on Russia. – Swimming in the afternoon' (2 August 1914; *D* 301/*TB* 543). This laconic entry is often cited as evidence of Kafka's political indifference, but it conceals a more complex story. That summer, Kafka had been preparing to radically change his life; he wanted to leave his insurance post and move to Berlin or Munich as a freelance writer. The war put an end to this plan. Although Kafka was put off by the military parades and patriotic speeches, in 1916 he made a determined effort to enlist, which was thwarted by his boss at the Insurance Institute, who insisted that he was indispensable at work. Kafka was furious and even threatened to resign; in a letter to Felice, he wrote that 'it would be my good fortune to become a soldier' (3 May 1915; *LF* 493/*B1* 133). Through the first-hand accounts of eastern Jewish refugees, his brothers-in-law and the many injured soldiers who descended on the Insurance Institute, Kafka must have had a clear sense of the gruesome reality of the war. So why was he so keen to enlist? As Kafka's biographer, Reiner Stach, argues, his desire to become a soldier was driven not by naïve patriotism but by a more basic motive – his urge to escape from the deadening routine of daily life, at whatever cost.[2]

1917–1924: illness, reflection, late happiness

Another major turning point in Kafka's life was the outbreak of the illness that would eventually kill him. In August 1917, he suffered a nocturnal haemorrhage; although he immediately suspected the worst, it took several months until he was formally diagnosed with tuberculosis. Faced with this situation, Kafka made some radical changes. Not only did he end the relationship with Felice Bauer, but he took a six-month break from work, during which he lived with his sister Ottla in the north Bohemian village of Zürau. During this time, he produced the so-called Zürau aphorisms – short, reflective pieces which marked a shift away from narrative fiction.

In the summer of 1919, Kafka got engaged again, this time to the twenty-seven-year-old Julie Wohryzek, the daughter of a Czech-Jewish synagogue servant. Kafka's parents tried to sabotage the match by hiring a private detective, who uncovered compromising stories about Julie's past, but in the end their marriage plans fell through for a more trivial reason: two days before the wedding, they failed to secure a joint flat and decided to postpone the wedding. Their relationship then became less close and eventually fell apart when, in the spring of 1920, Kafka met the Czech journalist and translator Milena Jesenská. Milena, who lived in Vienna, had translated Kafka's 'The Stoker' into Czech. She had married the Jewish literary critic Ernst Pollack against her father's will, but the marriage was on shaky grounds, and soon she and Kafka entered into an intense and passionate correspondence. On his way back from a spa break in Meran, Kafka spent four happy days with Milena in Vienna. She told her husband about the affair, but Kafka soon grew distant, seeing no future for the relationship.

Kafka's final – and arguably happiest – relationship was with the twenty-five-year-old Dora Diamant, whom he met in the summer of 1923 while on holiday in Müritz on the Baltic coast. Dora, who had broken away from her ultra-orthodox Hasidic family in Poland, worked for a Jewish holiday camp and was a member of a Zionist organization promoting the Hebrew language. She became Kafka's companion during the final stages of his illness. In the autumn of 1923, Kafka took the momentous step of moving away from Prague to live with Dora in Berlin. It was a happy and productive time, although high inflation devalued Kafka's pension and made their financial situation extremely strained. They relied on food parcels from Prague, and because of his declining health Kafka was increasingly tied to their flat. In March 1924, he was forced to leave Berlin and return home. At a clinic in Vienna it was confirmed that his tuberculosis had spread to the larynx.

Kafka spent his final weeks first in a sanatorium in Ortmann in Lower Austria and then in the quiet village of Kierling near Klosterneuburg. There he was initially able to undertake some excursions, but then his health quickly deteriorated. Talking, swallowing and breathing became a torture that was alleviated only by morphine injections. Kafka had been instructed not to talk (a common but pointless therapeutic measure at the time) and thus communicated with Dora and his friend Robert Klopstock in writing. In a letter, he asked Dora's father for permission to marry her, which was declined. He received visits from Max Brod, his sister Ottla, his brother-in-law Karl Hermann and his uncle Siegfried Löwy. In a poignantly optimistic letter written on the day before his death, he asked his parents to postpone their visit; its last sentence reads: 'So shall we not let it ride for the present, dear parents?' (2 June 1924; *LFFE* 415/*BE* 82). On 3 June, Kafka's breathing became so laboured that he asked Klopstock, a medicine student, for an overdose of morphine, allegedly saying to him: 'Kill me or else you're a murderer.' Kafka died on 3 June 1924 at around midday, with Dora by his side. He was buried in the Jewish cemetery in Straschnitz near Prague.

Chapter 2

Contexts

Like any writer, Kafka was influenced by his cultural, intellectual and political context. In his diaries and letters he often reflects on events and encounters; the resonances of these experiences in the fiction are subtler and less direct, which has led to the persistent cliché of Kafka as a solipsistic writer whose works bear little relation to their historical context. In the sections that follow, I will single out three configurations which shaped Kafka's life and times, outlining both the general situation and their specific, personal implications.

The modern city: avant-garde, mass culture, pathology

The early twentieth century was a time of rapid social change, technological modernization and artistic innovation. There was an unprecedented explosion of literary movements, and 'modernism' is at best an umbrella term for a variety of co-existing avant-garde movements. Expressionism, Symbolism, Art Nouveau, Dadaism and Futurism pursued contrasting and often conflicting agendas, but they all marked a move away from the tenets of realism and Naturalism, which had dominated the literature of the nineteenth century. Now the focus was no longer on the close, quasi-scientific observation of outside reality but on the depiction of inner states and psychological processes, of fantasies, dreams and desires. At the same time, the texts written around 1900 express a deep sense of crisis – the crisis of the individual lost in an increasingly complex, fragmented world, but also a crisis of language. Many modernist writers and thinkers, including the Austrian authors Hugo von Hofmannsthal and Robert Musil, questioned the ability of language – which by its nature is bound by conventions – to express authentic feelings and experiences. This led to a revived interest in mysticism as a way of overcoming the boundaries of the self and the rational limitations of human existence.

At the other end of the spectrum, the early twentieth century saw the emergence of urban mass culture: of music halls, variety theatres and, most importantly, of the cinema. Writing in the 1920s, German critic Siegfried Kracauer described these places of mass entertainment as 'temples of distraction', where office workers sought escape from the monotony of their daily lives as well as from a more existential sense of spiritual homelessness.

As Kracauer's comment implies, city life had its critics as well as its advocates. The many people who flocked to the city from the middle of the nineteenth century onwards were attracted primarily by its economic opportunities. Cities were great melting pots, facilitating social mobility and a gradual move towards greater equality in terms of class, gender and religion. In the early 1900s, women started to take up paid employment in larger numbers, particularly in offices. This brought with it more liberal attitudes towards sexual relationships, although bourgeois family structures generally remained intact, as did traditional moral values.

Compared with life in a village or small town, however, where the individual is part of a tight-knit community, cities are crowded, sprawling and anonymous; and often anonymity goes hand in hand with a lack of privacy, with a sense of exposure to the intrusive gaze of others. Many people found the thrill of the city irresistible, and many writers were inspired by the speed and excitement of urban life, but this aspect was also criticized and even pathologized. One of the buzzwords of the period was neurasthenia, a term coined by the American psychiatrist George M. Beard in his book *American Nervousness* (1880). Neurasthenia denotes a kind of nervous weakness, which manifests itself as general listlessness but also as a heightened, pathological sensitivity towards (urban) stimuli and impressions.

However, not everyone saw these developments as intrinsically negative. One of the first critics to analyse the social and psychological repercussions of the city was the German sociologist Georg Simmel. In his 1903 essay 'The Metropolis and Mental Life', he argues that the 'swift and continuous shift and external and internal stimuli' brings about an 'intensification of mental life', training the city-dweller to interact with people and things in a purely rational manner untainted by emotion.[1] Simmel praises this shift as an opportunity to break away from old modes of experience and adapt to the demands of the modern 'money economy', an abstract system of circulation and exchange. His findings are echoed, in more negative terms, by Max Weber, another founding father of modern sociology. Weber describes modern society as 'disenchanted' and dominated by the principles of rationality and efficiency. In his seminal study, *The Protestant Ethic and the Spirit of Capitalism* (1904–5), Weber argues that modern capitalism is in fact infused with Protestant values, which require individuals to forsake all worldly pleasures in order to dedicate themselves to economic success – a sign of God's grace. In modern capitalism, this Protestant concern for material wealth has turned into a 'shell as hard as steel' without a spiritual core.[2] Unlike his Protestant predecessor, modern 'bureaucratic man' lacks an inner sense of moral guidance and is hence solely dependent on the rules provided from the outside, by political institutions and other organisations.

Kafka's writings echo the sociological theories of the time. Many of his texts, such as *The Man who Disappeared*, revel in the fast pace of the city while also illustrating the danger of sensory overload, of the endless succession of disparate stimuli, which cannot be processed or unified. Josef K., in *The Trial*, embodies the ruthless striving for economic success described by Weber, which comes to supplant all other (moral) concerns. However, in his personal life Kafka sought to distance himself from the strains of modernity. Although he enjoyed city life – he was an enthusiastic cinema-goer – he was deeply attracted to the idea of a simpler, rural life. He intermittently did gardening work in a nursery outside Prague, and in 1917–18 he spent several months with his sister Ottla, who ran a farm in the Bohemian village of Zürau. As a reaction to the pressures of city life and industrialization, various alternative health movements emerged in the early twentieth century, ranging from vegetarianism and naturism to the promotion of looser, healthier clothing (especially for women) and different exercise regimes. Kafka was a vegetarian and followed a particular eating method known as Fletcherizing, whereby each mouthful was to be chewed thirty-two times. In addition, he rowed and swam and kept up a daily routine of gymnastic exercises. This healthy lifestyle notwithstanding, Kafka suffered from states of nervous exhaustion for most of his adult life, and long before he was diagnosed with tuberculosis he spent his vacations in sanatoriums, seeking to restore his strength.

Psychoanalysis and intergenerational conflict

Sociology was one of the formative discourses around 1900; another was psychoanalysis. Its founder, the Viennese doctor Sigmund Freud, set out to explore psychological processes and dynamics and the way the psyche is in turn shaped by external, familial and societal structures.

In 1900 Freud published *The Interpretation of Dreams*, which put psycho-analysis firmly on the cultural map of the period. In his writings, Freud addressed pathological conditions such as hysteria, neurosis and psychosis alongside 'mainstream' issues such as religion, family life and sexuality. A neurologist by training, Freud always insisted that psychoanalysis should be counted among the sciences, although arguably his greatest influence was within the arts. His writings explore the origins of creativity and the workings of the imagination, drawing parallels between the mechanisms at work in dreams and the structure of a literary text. Freud was widely read and often used examples from art and literature to illustrate his theories. His Oedipus complex, named after Sophocles' drama *Oedipus Rex*, is the most famous example; another is his essay on 'The Uncanny', which draws on the novella 'The Sandman' (1816) by the German Romantic writer E. T. A. Hoffmann. Indeed, Freud admitted early on that his case studies – his accounts of the treatment of particular patients – 'read like short stories and that, one might say, they lack the serious stamp of science'.[3]

This is not to say that Freud's theories were incompatible with scientific theories of his age. In an 1886 study, the Austrian physicist Ernst Mach argued that the self was not a stable, self-contained entity, but the product of a transitory stream of sensory impressions, stating categorically, 'The *self* is unsalvageable.' Freud, in his writings, gradually comes to develop a similarly decentred model of the self. For him, the psyche is the site of three conflicting forces: the id, the site of primitive drives and desire; the super-ego, a kind of psychological police force trying to uphold internalized moral values; and the ego, the 'reality principle', which tries to mediate between the two. If this balance is disturbed, neuroses and compulsions come to control the subject. Freud's goal as a therapist was to enable his patients to confront their uncon-scious motivations and hence regain control over them. As he famously wrote, 'Where id was, there ego shall be.'[4]

Modernist authors responded to Freud's theories with a mixture of fascination and suspicion, and Kafka was no exception. Kafka's texts cannot be understood without some reference to psychoanalytic theory, and yet it would be reductive to use psychoanalysis as the key to unlock their 'hidden' meaning. As we will see in subsequent chapters, whenever Kafka draws on psychoanalytic models, he adapts and subverts them in creative ways.

Unlike many modernist authors, Kafka never underwent psychotherapy, nor did he read psychoanalytic theories in a systematic way. In a letter to his friend Willy Haas, Kafka describes his attitude towards Freud as a mixture of ignorance and admiration: 'I'm sure one can read unprecedented things by

Freud. Unfortunately I know little by him and much by his pupils and for that reason I only have a great, but empty respect for him' (19 July 1912; *B1* 162). Psychoanalysis was discussed in the literary journals Kafka read, in Berta Fanta's philosophical salon, which he attended intermittently, and in the reading circle he had formed with Brod and Felix Weltsch. Another point of contact was through literary criticism. In a letter of 1917, Kafka mentions an interpretation of *The Metamorphosis* by Freud's pupil Wilhelm Stekel. Although he dismissively describes Stekel as someone 'who reduces Freud to small change' (23 September 1917; *LFFE* 145/*B3* 327), Kafka's letter underlines an important point: one of the reasons why modernist writers were interested in psychoanalysis was because psychoanalysts were in turn interested in them, applying their findings to literary texts.

Kafka respected psychoanalytic theory for its intellectual contribution to modernist debate, but was sceptical about the project of psychological (self-) analysis, which he saw as too simplistic to reflect the complexity of human experience. In 1917 he notes: 'There is no such thing as observation of the inner world, as there is of the outer world. Psychology is probably, taken as a whole, a form of anthropomorphism, a nibbling at our own limits' (*ON* 14/*NS II* 32).

A more personal connection with psychoanalysis was forged through Kafka's acquaintance with the charismatic but controversial psychoanalyst Otto Gross. Kafka met Gross in 1917 and was enthusiastic about Gross's plan to found a new periodical, *Journal for the Fight against the Will to Power*. Gross had made the headlines in 1913, when his own father, Hans Gross, had him sectioned in a mental institution for his drug abuse and 'anti-bourgeois' lifestyle. Hans Gross was an eminent law professor, whose lectures Kafka had attended as a student in Prague. Following widespread protest, Otto Gross was released again; his story resonated with many young writers and intellectuals, for it epitomized the father–son conflict – the son's brutal oppression by the father – which was a prominent theme in Expressionist literature and in Kafka's own writings.

But Gross's story would have also resonated with Kafka for more personal reasons. Kafka lived with his parents for nearly all his life and often commented on the oppressive nature of family relations and in particular on his difficult relationship with his father, Hermann. His most detailed account of this relationship can be found in the so-called 'Letter to his Father' ('Brief an den Vater'), which he wrote in 1919 but never actually gave to his father. This long letter is the closest Kafka came to writing his autobiography. It traces his life with his father from his early childhood up to the time of writing; the recurring theme is how Hermann Kafka's dominating presence stunted his son's development and made him feel perpetually inadequate.

Kafka's letter paints the picture of a petty tyrant, a hypocrite who imposes on his children rules that he himself cheerfully ignores. One key scene is Kafka's memory of being locked out of the flat at night as a young child and forced to stand outside in the cold, because he had cried and disrupted his parents' sleep; another is the father's insensitive advice to his sixteen-year-old son that he should visit a brothel to overcome his sexual inhibitions. As Kafka recounts in his letter, in the eyes of his son the father remained unsullied by his own crude suggestion, 'a married man, unspotted, high above these things ... So since the world consisted of only you and me – an idea that seemed quite obvious to me – then the purity of the world came to an end with you, and on account of your advice the filth began with me' (*M* 132–3/*NS II* 203–4). The letter is full of vividly remembered episodes, which Kafka uses to build an almost mythical image of his father's absolute authority. In this passage, Kafka creates an absolute divide between the pure father and his filthy son; in another, he mentally exaggerates the father's size until his body stretches across the entire globe (*M* 136/*NS II* 210). Throughout the letter, then, Kafka's condemnation of his father is intertwined with a sense of admiration. Hermann Kafka embodies a model of masculinity – physically, professionally and especially as a husband and father – to which his son felt he could never aspire. Kafka dreaded the prospects of marriage and fatherhood, and he yet regarded them as the highest goals of all.

Kafka's 'Letter to his Father' is an ambivalent document, situated somewhere between confessional writing and fiction. The image it paints of Hermann Kafka is monstrous, terrifying; if this was Kafka's attempt to work through his childhood traumas, the letter might arguably have had the opposite effect, cementing his sense of disempowerment. And yet the letter is also a rhetorical masterpiece, which shows Kafka's legal training – his eye for detail and his dialectical method of arguing, of anticipating the opponent's position. Though most of it is a monologue, the ending comes with a twist, for here Kafka lets the father reply to his accusations, allowing him to debunk his son's claims. Kafka here seems to surrender control of his narrative, and yet this move might in fact be a double twist, an advocate's trick. By putting words into his father's mouth, Kafka becomes his ventriloquist and the father a mere puppet in this Oedipal drama.

Kafka's Prague: multiculturalism, Judaism, Zionism

When we think of the European cultural centres around 1900, we think of cities such as Paris and London, Vienna and Berlin. Prague does not usually feature on this cultural map, and yet it was a unique place, a multilingual and multi-ethnic city informed by growing nationalist tensions. Around 1900, Prague was still relatively small and provincial, but its population was growing rapidly; in 1900 it had around 200,000 inhabitants, but by 1925 it had grown to over 700,000. Up to 1918, Prague was part of the Habsburg Empire, a multi-ethnic state governed by a small German-speaking elite. As a result of a big influx from the surrounding Bohemia from the middle of the nineteenth century onwards, however, its Czech population was growing steadily; in 1848 two thirds of the population spoke German, but by 1880 this share had decreased to 14 per cent and by 1910 had halved again to less than 7 per cent. At the same time, the Czech nationalist movement was gaining in support, putting the German-speaking minority under growing pressure.

The power balance in Prague radically changed after the First World War, which marked the end of the Habsburg monarchy and the dissolution of its multi-ethnic empire. In October 1918 the republic of Czechoslovakia was founded, with Prague as its capital. In 1939 the city was invaded by the Nazis, who made it the capital of the newly founded 'Protectorate of Bohemia and Moravia'. Of the approximately 120,000 Jewish people who lived in Bohemia at the time, about 78,000 were murdered by the Nazis; the victims included Kafka's three sisters, Elli, Valli and Ottla.

Despite, or perhaps because of, its relative isolation and internal tensions, Prague was a particularly productive place for writers. Kafka and his friend Max Brod were among a small but successful group of German-speaking (predominantly Jewish) authors who found themselves in a linguistically and culturally isolated minority, a situation which arguably shaped their writing. Many of the more prominent Prague authors, however, left the city early on. Apart from Rainer Maria Rilke, they include Gustav Meyrink (author of the fantastical novel *The Golem*), the Expressionist Franz Werfel, the writer and illustrator Alfred Kubin and the journalist Egon Erwin Kisch. Kafka was one of the few who remained in Prague almost throughout his life, though his attitude towards the city was deeply ambivalent. As he wrote to his friend Oskar Pollak: 'Prague doesn't let go. . . . This old crone has claws' (20 December 1902; *LFFE* 5/*B1* 17).

In his diary, Kafka reflected on the situation faced by German-speaking Prague writers by drawing up a 'character sketch of the literature of small peoples'. His list includes features such as 'Conflict', 'Absence of principles', 'Minor themes' and 'Connection with politics' (27 December 1911; *D* 150–1/ *TB* 326). Gilles Deleuze and Félix Guattari developed Kafka's model in their 1975 study *Kafka: Toward a Minor Literature*. As they argue, in 'minor literature' (by which they mean literature written in a major language but from a minority position) even the smallest individual concern is political and 'everything takes on a collective value'.[5] In Kafka's case, this linguistic minority status was combined with an ethnic one. The majority of German-speakers in Prague in the early 1900s were of Jewish descent; in the climate of growing nationalism they were in a particularly precarious position and were often the target of covert discrimination or open hostility.

Judaism at Kafka's time was not a coherent movement, but was internally divided. Many European Jews of the older generation were committed to the project of assimilation, of integrating into mainstream Western society. Kafka's generation, in contrast, responded critically to the assimilatory aspirations of their parents. They looked to the Yiddish-speaking Jews of Eastern Europe as a model for spiritual renewal, and motivated by the rising tide of anti-Semitism across Europe, they turned to Zionism for an alternative perspective. The Zionist movement campaigned for the foundation of a Jewish nation state in Palestine, which culminated in the foundation of the state of Israel in 1948. In the early twentieth century, however, Zionism was not widely endorsed by the Jewish population of Western Europe; many people regarded the idea of a Jewish nation state as unnecessary or utopian or – as in the case of their Eastern European counterparts – as a rebellion against a Jewish exile imposed by God. Thus many intellectuals argued instead for a renaissance of Jewish culture within Western society, a renaissance which should be achieved particularly through the medium of literature.

Many of Kafka's closest friends – such as his school friend Hugo Bergmann and, later, Max Brod, Felix Weltsch and Oskar Baum – were supporters of Zionism. In Prague, the movement was active through the student organization 'Bar Kochba', which organized lectures by prominent speakers such as the philosopher Martin Buber. In these lectures, which Kafka attended, Buber contrasted the assimilated urban lifestyle of Western European Jews with the authentic, rural lifestyle of their Eastern European counterparts. This opposition between Eastern and Western Jewish traditions is a recurring theme in Kafka's letters and diaries, though his attitude towards Judaism, Zionism and his own Jewish identity remains complex and ambivalent. In the 'Letter to his Father', Kafka criticizes his father for having allowed his own Jewish heritage to become so diluted that there was nothing left to pass on to his son. His own diary accounts of visiting the synagogue and of his nephew's circumcision betray a palpable sense of detachment, but Kafka tried to make up for his lack of religious roots. A turning point was his acquaintance with a Yiddish theatre troupe, whose performances Kafka attended in the winter of 1911–12. He befriended the actors and even helped raise funds for the group by giving a public talk on the Yiddish language. He read widely about Jewish history, culture and literature, including several collections of Hasidic folk tales. During the First World War, he helped support Eastern European refugees who were passing through Prague, and in 1916 he visited the Rabbi of Belz in Marienbad with his friend Georg Langer. Langer, a Czech-speaking Jew from Prague, had himself lived in the Hasidic community in Belz. Kafka's account of the Rabbi, who had fled to Marienbad from the Russian army, reveals a mixture of curiosity, doubt and fascination.

From 1914 onwards, Kafka taught himself Hebrew and also took intermittent lessons. Although he regarded the Zionist fervour of his friends with slight suspicion, he attended various Zionist events and in 1923 seriously considered emigrating to Palestine. This plan was aborted because of his declining health; in the end he moved to Berlin instead, where he continued his Hebrew studies and also took courses on the Talmud.

Kafka's engagement with Judaism, Zionism and the Yiddish culture of Eastern Europe was recurrent but intermittent; it testifies to his fascination with a tradition that continued to elude him. In a letter to Milena Jesenká, he emphatically defined himself as a Western Jew:

> We both know, after all, enough typical examples of Western Jews. I am as far as I know the most typical Western Jew among them. This means, expressed with exaggeration, that not one calm second is granted me, nothing is granted me, everything has to be earned, not only the present and the future, but the past too.   (November 1920; *LM* 174/*BM* 294)

Paradoxically, then, Kafka's engagement with his Jewish roots results in a sense of rootlessness. His literary texts contain numerous, mostly implicit, references to Jewish tradition, through motifs and storylines, but also through underlying models of writing, reading and interpretation. Ultimately, however, for Kafka religious experience could only be grasped in the negative, in a state of elusiveness and withdrawal. As he wrote to Brod after visiting the Rabbi of Belz together with Georg Langer: 'L[anger] tries to find or thinks he finds a deeper meaning in all this; I think that the deeper meaning is that there is none, and in my opinion this is quite enough' (mid July 1916; *LFFE* 122/*B2* 180).

Works

Early works

Although Kafka started writing in the middle of the 1890s, he later destroyed many of the stories, diaries and letters he had written before 1912. Only a handful of these earliest texts have survived; the most substantial are the prose narratives 'Description of a Struggle' and 'Wedding Preparations in the Country' – both of them unpublished during Kafka's lifetime – and his first book, a collection of short prose texts called *Meditation* (1912). These early texts have received much less attention than his later works, for critics have often argued that they are not representative of Kafka's 'mature' style. However, these early texts deserve our attention for two reasons. First, they show a less familiar Kafka, an author who experiments more freely with different narrative techniques and whose texts reflect the influence of avant-garde movements such as Decadence, Impressionism and Expressionism, but also of the 'new' medium of film. Second, although these early texts may strike us as quite different from Kafka's more famous works, they contain many of the themes and stylistic features which also define Kafka's later texts; in fact, there is a strong sense of continuity from his earliest works all the way through to his last.

'Description of a Struggle'

'Description of a Struggle' ('Beschreibung eines Kampfes'), on which Kafka worked intermittently between 1904 and 1910, is a complex, multi-layered text which skilfully interweaves different narrative strands and perspectives. At a party, the nameless first-person narrator meets an acquaintance, who tells him about his sweetheart. They leave together and wander through the nocturnal city. In the middle section, the plot takes a turn towards the surreal. The narrator leaps on to his acquaintance's shoulders, riding him like a horse, and gets him to take him out of the city and into a forest. There he meets an extraordinarily fat man, who tells the narrator about his encounter with another character, the 'supplicant'. At the end of this middle part, the fat man is swept down a waterfall, and the plot returns to the original narrator and his acquaintance, who continue their conversation while walking through the forest.

Most of the characters are referred to by epithet rather than by proper name, a technique commonly used in Expressionist drama, where character types represent more general social dynamics. Expressionist plays often revolve around conflict – between fathers and sons, between social classes, or between the generations. As the title indicates, this motif is also central in 'Description of a Struggle', but here struggle does not take on an explicitly social or political dimension but remains mostly on a psychological level. In the first section, the introvert narrator tries in vain to escape from his vivacious, outgoing acquaintance, but in the second part, he suddenly gains the upper hand when he mounts his acquaintance and assumes his cheerful indifference: 'I laughed and trembled with courage' (*CSS* 21/*NS I* 73). Here as elsewhere, the relationship between characters is antagonistic but also unstable and subject to sudden reversal.

'Struggle', then, is a key word of the text, but the title also points to a stylistic feature. The term 'description' suggests a conventionally realist narrative, and in fact the story is the only one of Kafka's texts which is set recognizably in the Prague of his time, as is indicated by street names and other landmarks. However, this realist setting forms the backdrop of an increasingly bizarre story in which the boundaries between reality and imagination become blurred. Thus, the narrator is able to alter the surrounding landscape to suit his mood, and the characters in the middle section, the fat man and the supplicant, are less real figures than figments of the narrator's imagination. Revealingly, the story becomes more dreamlike as the narrator leaves the city for the Laurenziberg (Petřín), a recreational area in the middle of Prague. While the city is the realm of social relations, nature gives rise to the irrational impulses of the mind. As we will see, the contrast between city and countryside is a recurring theme in Kafka's early writings, both in *Meditation* and in 'Wedding Preparations in the Country'.

'Wedding Preparations in the Country'

'Wedding Preparations in the Country' ('Hochzeitsvorbereitungen auf dem Lande', 1906–7; 1909) is a more conventionally realist text than 'Description of a Struggle'. Eduard Raban, a young man, is engaged to a girl called Betty, and he travels from his flat in the city to the countryside to visit her. The text – Kafka referred to it as a novel – is unfinished. It breaks off just as Raban arrives in the village after dark; Betty herself never gets to make an appearance. The actual plot is thus very simple. Large parts of the third-person narrative are taken up with descriptions of the city and the people Raban encounters on his journey. The text opens with an urban street scene, which evocatively describes passers-by, their appearance, body language and behaviour. All this is described from a detached perspective, which reflects the influence of realist novels such as Gustave Flaubert's *Sentimental Education* (1869), which was one of Kafka's favourite books.

However, the text not only describes the outside world but gives us detailed insights into the protagonist's mind. Raban feels distant from his fiancée – he cannot even remember the colour of her eyes – and dreads the prospect of the visit. This fear is intermingled with a visceral dislike of the countryside. In contrast to the vibrant city, the countryside is silent, dark, impenetrable – and yet strangely alluring:

> behind the poplars on the far side of the railway track there was the landscape, so massive that it took one's breath. Was it a dark view through a clearing or was it a forest, was it a pond or a house in which people were already asleep, was it a church steeple or a ravine between the hills? Nobody must dare to go there, but who could restrain himself? (*CSS* 67/*NS I* 36–7)

Raban's ambivalent response to the rural landscape mirrors his attitude towards his fiancée. Marriage is an unknown territory that has yet to be mapped out and which threatens to engulf the protagonist but which, like the countryside, is not without appeal. Raban is one of the first in a succession of bachelors who populate Kafka's texts. For them – as for Kafka himself – marriage is a deeply ambivalent prospect: a state associated with companionship and stability, but also with the straitjacket of responsibility.

Raban spends much of his time agonizing about his visit and tries to come up with plans to defer it. Rather than going himself, he fantasizes that he could send a substitute – his 'clothed body', who could tend to his social obligations while he himself stayed in bed: 'As I lie in bed I assume the shape of a big beetle, a stag beetle or a cockchafer, I think' (*CSS* 56/*NS I* 17–18). In *The Metamorphosis*, this motif – the transformation into a beetle – will be promoted from fantasy to reality, losing its air of cosy escapism in the process.

The early diaries: a creative laboratory

As these two examples show, the young Kafka experimented with a wide variety of styles and literary techniques, oscillating between closely observed realism and an inward-looking, at points dreamlike or surrealist, mode of writing. Both of these elements are also present in another textual medium that plays a major role in Kafka's literary development: his diaries.

About half of his surviving diaries, which in the German critical edition run to over a thousand pages, date from the years up to 1912. His diary helped Kafka the aspiring author to establish a writing routine, building up a sense of momentum, which he hoped to carry over into his creative writing. The diaries' main purpose is not the recording of daily events; rather, they are exercises in observation and reflection. Kafka comments on his inner state and on his literary work, noting influences and inspirations. In addition, he delves deep into the pre-rational part of his mind when recording dreams, daydreams or semi-conscious thoughts and fantasies. Although Kafka's prose style is sober and controlled, his creative approach bears some resemblance to the Surrealist technique of *écriture automatique*, or automatic writing, which was meant to loosen the mind's conscious control over the writing process.

Inward-looking reflection is one important component of the early diaries, but they are also exercises in observation. Kafka describes the sights and people he encounters in his day-to-day life, but especially on his travels to other parts of Bohemia, to Germany, Italy and France. A particular source of inspiration is a visiting Yiddish theatre group, led by the actor Jizchak Löwy, whose performances Kafka regularly attended in the autumn and winter of 1911–12. He records his impressions in great detail, highlighting nonverbal elements such as the actors' body language and facial expressions. These diary entries anticipate his later literary texts, where gestures play a central role, adding an additional though often impenetrable layer of meaning to the narrative.

Kafka was, as his friends testify, a very visually oriented person with a keen interest in the arts. Indeed, he was also a talented draftsman who, as Max Brod recalls, as a student used to draw in the margins of his lecture notes. Many of his iconic pen-and-ink drawings of androgynous figures captured in expressive poses date from his student years (see Fig. 2), and drawing remained one of his

2 Some of Kafka's drawings

pastimes, perhaps as a counterpoint to writing. Little sketches, usually of people, can be found in his notebooks, diaries, letters and postcards. Another of Kafka's great interests was photography, although this interest was less practical. While he probably did not own a camera, he was a keen viewer and collector of photographs, as becomes particularly clear in his correspondence with Felice Bauer, where he displays an almost insatiable hunger for photographs of his beloved. As his letters reveal, photographs for Kafka were rarely straightforward, but offered puzzling and at times even alienating perspectives on reality; despite the unsettling nature of photography, however, Kafka contrasted it favourably with another, even more recent, visual medium. On a business trip to the Bohemian town of Friedland, Kafka visited the Kaiser Panorama, a slide show of three-dimensional, or 'stereoscopic', photographs. In his diary, the account of this visit sparks a comparison between film and photography: 'The pictures [are] more alive than in the cinema because they offer the eye all the repose of reality. The cinema communicates the restlessness of its motion to the things pictured in it; the eye's repose would seem to be more important' (*D* 430/*TB* 937). Kafka was an avid cinema-goer, and in his diaries he tries to capture particular scenes from his cinema visits, though often these impressions prove to be too fast-moving and elusive. In the early twentieth century, writers took inspiration from the new medium of film, trying to write in a cinematic way, for instance through the literary 'montage' of contrasting images. As Kafka's diary account of the Kaiser Panorama shows, however, he remained sceptical about the medium's literary potential. For him, the static nature of photography was not a weakness but an advantage, as it offered scope for a more contemplative, controlled mode of perception. In order to depict the complexity of modern life, the writer needs to be able to decelerate or even arrest the stream of impressions into distinct images, and this is precisely what Kafka does in his fiction.

This process can be traced in 'Wedding Preparations in the Country'. The opening street scene exists in three versions, for in 1909, two years after abandoning the project, Kafka returned to the text and attempted two further beginnings. While the earliest version depicts a constantly changing scene, an amalgam of vehicles and people who are sketched out without much detail, in the third version, this fluidity is replaced by a succession of self-contained narrative 'frames'. Anticipating his own comments on the Kaiser Panorama, Kafka 'zooms in' on a few pedestrians, each of whom is given a separate paragraph, but this last version is also the shortest and does not develop beyond the opening scene. After the third attempt, Kafka abandoned his novel project for good and tried his hand at shorter prose forms instead.

Meditation

With *Meditation* (*Betrachtung*), his first book to be published, Kafka takes stock of his literary achievements to date. Published in 1912, it assembles eighteen short prose texts, the earliest of which date back to at least 1906; four of them are excerpts from 'Description of a Struggle', while others are taken from the diaries. The texts are extremely diverse in form, style and subject-matter. While some are short stories in the more conventional sense, others barely have a plot or recognizable characters. The volume's title sums up the two main components of Kafka's early work. The German *Betrachtung* means 'contemplation' or 'meditation', but also 'observation'. Both meanings are reflected throughout the collection, which contains closely observed scenes alongside more abstract, reflective pieces.

Although Kafka felt ambivalent towards his first book, unsure whether the short texts he had selected really deserved publication, *Meditation* fitted the literary climate of the time rather well. Short prose writing was a thriving genre in the early twentieth century, when authors experimented with new narrative forms and techniques. The fast pace of urban life resulted in a fragmented mode of perception, which defied the comprehensive, unified representation typical of nineteenth-century realism. But do the short prose texts merely reflect the disparity of modern life? In his essay 'The Small Form' (1926), the Viennese author Alfred Polgar concedes that the small form may well be a 'necessary effect of a shortness of breath', but he nonetheless defends this mode of writing as 'thoroughly appropriate to the role today demanded of writing', arguing that short texts suit 'the tension and need of the time' better than 'written skyscrapers'.[1] This claim is echoed by the critic Walter Benjamin; for him, short prose fosters a much-needed sensitivity for 'austere, delicate, faceless things'.[2] Although *Meditation* appeared over a decade earlier, it chimes with these remarks. Its texts often revolve around brief encounters, transient moods and inconspicuous details which would normally go unnoticed. Many of the pieces are deliberately inconsequential, and the narrative momentum peters out without a climax or resolution; others do not even have a plot but are more akin to thought experiments, often involving 'if – then' constructions. In their 'smallness' and apparent simplicity, the texts of *Meditation* draw attention to the 'austere, delicate, faceless things' surrounding us. By doing so, however, they pose much larger questions about the human condition, pointing to an underlying mood of uncertainty and crisis. This is illustrated by the two shortest pieces of the collection, which appear close to the end of the volume. While 'Wish to Become a Red Indian' ('Wunsch, Indianer zu werden') describes a sense of movement, 'Trees' ('Die Bäume') thematizes rootedness and stability – or so it seems. In fact, both texts undo their own premise.

'Wish to Become a Red Indian' is made up of one single sentence describing a wishful fantasy. The narrator longs to be a Red Indian riding on a horse, but then this image is gradually stripped of all distinguishing features:

> Oh to be a Red Indian, ready in an instant, riding a swift horse, aslant in the air, thundering again and again over the thundering earth, until you let the spurs go, for there weren't any spurs, until you cast off the reins, for there weren't any reins, and you scarcely saw the land ahead of you as close-cropped scrub, being already without horse's neck and horse's head!   (*M* 15/*DL* 32–3)

Stories and films about the American Wild West, about cowboys and Indians, were very popular in Kafka's time. They conveyed a sense of adventure, of a more authentic life untouched by social conventions. So the figure of the Red Indian provides a tangible cultural reference point, but this premise is then dismantled as the ride becomes more and more abstract; the rider abandons spurs, reins and eventually even his horse, moving across a landscape that is barely visible. The wish to *become* a Red Indian is realized as a process of abstraction, a gradual stripping away of the features that make up this identity. The text uses a realist pretext to get started but gradually abandons this vehicle as the narrative becomes self-perpetuating. What remains is a sense of pure movement: a movement across space, but also the movement of the text. The smoothness of the 'close-cropped scrub' resembles the blank page over which the pen can glide freely – but as the last realist reference point is abandoned, the text comes to a halt.

The even shorter piece 'Trees' responds to 'Wish to Become a Red Indian', carrying on its momentum while also stalling it. It starts with 'For' ('Denn'), as if in response to a claim or question; this opening gives it a sense of immediacy but also of instability:

> For we are like tree-trunks in the snow. They seem to rest smoothly on the surface [*liegen sie glatt auf*], and with a little nudge you could push them away. No, that can't be done, for they are connected firmly to the ground. But look, even that is only seeming.   (*M* 15/*DL* 33)

Whereas 'Wish to Become a Red Indian' consists of one long sentence, which reflects the speed of the ride, 'Trees' is made up of four short sentences, which make it more measured, but also more halting. The text elaborates on the image of tree trunks in the snow in three stages. It starts with a superficial first impression, the way this sight would appear to an observer with no prior knowledge of trees and their roots, and then counters this with what could be described as the common-sense view. The final sentence, however, overthrows this seemingly clear-cut opposition of illusion and reality. In a direct address, the reader is told that the second interpretation is itself just an illusion. The argument seems to have come full circle, and yet the final claim does not explicitly reinstate the first but merely discards the second.

This play with depth and surface, truth and appearance has a dizzying effect. Although the text deals with an apparently stable subject-matter, it creates its own destabilizing momentum. Once we have reached the puzzling conclusion, we find ourselves returning to the beginning. What does it mean that we are 'like' tree trunks in the snow? If the text is intended as a kind of allegory, it offers no clear lesson or conclusion. As in 'Wish to Become a Red Indian', any sense of certainty is eroded by the textual momentum. Although as readers – as human beings – we search for meaning and stability, this is overridden, both texts imply, by the flight of the imagination. This flight can be liberating, but it can also produce destabilizing uncertainty.

'Trees' and 'Wish to Become a Red Indian' exemplify several of the core features of *Meditation*. Many of Kafka's early texts seem straightforward at first glance but, like the tree trunks, they have hidden depths. Often events are recounted in the conditional mode, lending them a hypothetical character, while elsewhere reality seamlessly merges into fantasy. Some texts use the impersonal pronoun 'one' or the collective 'we', thus drawing the reader into their ruminations. Some pieces are left open-ended; in others the ending undermines what has come before. On the whole, *Meditation* makes for a fragmented and slightly vertiginous reading experience, requiring the reader to reassess his/her position in relation to each individual text.

The stories of *Meditation* oscillate between movement and stasis. Stationary observers turn into *flâneurs*, whereas characters who have wandered the city return to the quiet of their home. Walking the city is one way of escaping the monotony of life; another escape route leads into the world of fantasy and imagination, but both strategies can be disorienting. Indeed, many of Kafka's protagonists feel uncertain, alienated from themselves and their surroundings.

A case in point is the protagonist of 'The Passenger' ('Der Fahrgast'), who is 'utterly uncertain of my status in this world, in this city, in my family' (*M* 12/ *DL* 27). The movement of the tram on which he is travelling embodies this instability – but then the mood changes when his gaze is captured by a girl. She appears 'as distinct to me as if I had run my hands over her' (*M* 12/*DL* 27), and what follows is an invasively detailed description of her body. This mood change is typical of Kafka's early writings, where characters are suddenly propelled out of self-consciousness by a sight that captures their attention. The city is a space of encounters, some erotically charged, others more sinister.

In 'Unmasking a Confidence-Man' ('Entlarvung eines Bauernfängers'), the protagonist nearly falls prey to the advances of a confidence trickster. In 'The Runners' ('Die Vorüberlaufenden'), on the other hand, the sight of one man being pursued by another does not trigger any response in the onlooker, who simply muses on the possible reasons behind the chase. Unable to decide on one interpretation, he does nothing; here as elsewhere, reflection gets in the way of action. This text is not recounted from a personal perspective but involves an impersonal construction ('When one is going for a stroll along a lane at night ...' (*M* 12/*DL* 26)), which lends the story a hypothetical dimension.

This construction is used in several texts. In 'The Sudden Stroll' ('Der plötzliche Spaziergang'), the spontaneous decision to go for a walk after the house has been locked for the night produces a sense of freedom and elation. As the text concludes: 'All this is further reinforced if at this late hour you go and look up a friend to see how he is doing' (*M* 8/*DL* 18). Leaving one's home for a walk through the city harbours the prospect of sociality. The opposite movement – from the bustle of the city to the loneliness of the home – is described in 'The Small Businessman' ('Der Kaufmann') and 'The Way Home' ('Der Nachhauseweg'). In the latter, the ambulatory narrator feels at one with his surroundings on his brisk walk through the city, but once he arrives back home his mood suddenly changes: 'Only when I enter my room, I'm a little thoughtful, but without having found anything worth being thoughtful about as I came upstairs. It doesn't help me much to open the window wide, nor that music is still playing in the garden' (*M* 11/*DL* 25–6). In the solitude of the room, in the absence of outside stimulation, the self turns out to be an empty shell, and even the window, which in other stories provides a connection to the outside world, cannot fill this void.

This inner emptiness, which contrasts with the bustle outside, is a spectre which haunts several protagonists. One of the most poignant texts in the collection is the short piece 'The Bachelor's Distress' ('Das Unglück des Junggesellen'). It describes the lonely life of an old bachelor who, in times of illness, is forced to 'look for weeks at the empty room' (*M* 9/*DL* 21). Once again, this situation is presented as a thought experiment. The narrator tries to imagine what it must be like to lead such a life, and concludes, 'That is how it will be, only that in reality it will be you yourself standing there, today and later, with a body and a real head, and so with a brow too, to strike with your hand' (*M* 9/*DL* 21). This text forms a counterpart to 'Wish to Become a Red Indian'. While in the latter physical reality, including the horse's head, is gradually discarded, in 'The Bachelor's Distress' it is emphatically reaffirmed. Here, the real head, which is struck with a real hand, links this imaginary future self to the narrator's – and the reader's – actual body in the present. Kafka's thought experiments are more abstract and multi-layered than conventional stories, but they can also be surprisingly immediate, forcing us to confront our own response to a particular situation.

Most of the texts in *Meditation* are set in the city, but as a counterpoint the collection also includes stories set in the countryside, most notably the opening piece, 'Children on the Highway' ('Kinder auf der Landstraße'). Here, nature stands for a more authentic, idyllic existence. The text has a dreamlike atmosphere. On a summer evening, the young narrator sits on the swing in his parents' garden, idly watching the people who pass his house on their way home from work in the fields. He (or she – the narrator's gender is not spelled out) also follows with his eyes the flight of birds before he goes inside for dinner.

This opening bears some resemblance to the city texts of *Meditation*, where a solitary observer watches the bustle outside his window, but here the setting is idyllic, almost paradisiacal, and the young protagonist displays none of the anxiety of Kafka's city dwellers. The child moves seamlessly from solitude to company when, after dinner, he is called out by his friends, who have gathered outside the house. The domestic scene turns into a nocturnal adventure as the children run down the country lane, daring each other to jump into ditches. The narrative is punctuated by short dialogues in which the children spur each other on. The repeated imperative 'Come on!' conveys boundless energy and momentum; indeed, 'nothing could have stopped us' (*M* 5/*DL* 12). In this middle section, the narrative perspective shifts from 'I' to 'we' (and also the impersonal 'one'); the children have formed their own community apart from the adult world. This involves role play – they become exotic animals, soldiers and Red Indians – and singing: 'When your voice joins in with others, it's like being drawn along by a fish-hook' (*M* 5/*DL* 13). This sense of community is an ideal to which Kafka will rarely if ever return, although the community-building power of song is revisited in his very last story, 'Josefine, the Singer or The Mouse People' (1924). However, just as 'Children on the Highway' opens with the solitary child in the garden, it also ends on a more individualistic note. When the other children return back home, the narrator sets off on a journey towards the big city – home to people, who, as village legend has it, do not sleep. In this he might be inspired by the sight of an illuminated train that is passing in the distance. From the self-contained paradise of the garden, the story moves into the open country, and then leaves its protagonist as he embarks on a journey into the unknown.

Several motifs from the opening story are picked up again in the collection's concluding piece, 'Unhappiness' ('Unglücklichsein'). Like 'Children on the Highway', this is a substantial story told by a first-person narrator. Once again, Kafka returns to the figure of the lonely bachelor, but this time with a surreal twist. In a state of inner turmoil, the first-person narrator is pacing his room, which stretches out before him like a 'racecourse' (*M* 15/*DL* 33). As in 'Wish to Become a Red Indian', the dynamism of this movement is conveyed by one long sentence, which makes up the first paragraph. Initially, the narrator is absorbed by his own unhappiness, but then he is stirred out of this state when a child enters his room 'as a little ghost' (*M* 15/*DL* 34) – a cryptic formulation, which leaves the identity of this visitor tantalizingly ambiguous: is this a real child, a 'real' ghost, or a figment of the narrator's imagination?

The narrator's ensuing exchange with his young visitor is vague and incoherent, resembling an inner monologue rather than a real conversation. The narrator introduces himself and enquires whether his guest really wanted to see him, but then accuses the child of being late. He worries that his neighbours might find out about his visitor, but then, in the middle of a rather tense exchange, abruptly turns away to light a candle and sits at the table as if he were alone. Finally, he leaves his room and has a conversation with another tenant on the stairs, whom he tells about his ghostly visitor while declaring: 'Do you actually think I believe in ghosts, then? But what good is this not believing to me?' (*M* 18/*DL* 38).

'Unhappiness' oscillates between inside and outside, imagination and reality. When pacing his room, the narrator is drawn towards the depth of his mirror, and this motif is taken up in the ensuing conversation with the child, to whom the narrator remarks: 'Your nature is mine. And if I'm acting kindly towards you by nature, then you shouldn't act otherwise either' (*M* 17/*DL* 37). The child – whose gender remains uncertain – might be a figment of the narrator's imagination, but s/he is also his doppelgänger or alter ego, perhaps embodying his own childhood self. With the motif of the child, 'Unhappiness' refers back to the very first story. Whereas 'Children on the Highway' describes a summer idyll, 'Unhappiness' is set in a bleak November night. Childhood, a time of freedom and community, returns at the end of *Meditation* as a ghostly spectre, embodying not happy memories but the dark sides of the narrator's mind. As he says to his neighbour, 'The real fear is the fear of the cause of the apparition. And that fear remains' (*M* 18/*DL* 38–9).

Read in conjunction, the pieces of *Meditation* tell a coming-of-age story, a story of maturation and decline. The happy child leaves his village for the city to become a lonely bachelor. That said, just as 'Children on the Highway' contains various motifs – such as the figure of the Red Indian and the observation of people passing by – which recur in subsequent texts, so the move from the village to the city, from childhood to adulthood, is one the young narrator makes consciously. What attracts him to the city is the fact that it is inhabited by people who never sleep. These people, 'fools' (*M* 5/*DL* 14), are the characters populating Kafka's texts, in the early writings and beyond. His works are full of bachelors, dreamers and *flâneurs* who might not sleep soundly, but whose unhappy lives offer a fertile ground for Kafka's literary imagination. For Kafka, a lifelong insomniac, the night was the time of inspiration. This, as we will see, is nowhere more evident than in 'The Judgement', his literary breakthrough, where the familiar turns uncanny, and where childhood memories offer no protection against the terrors of adult life.

'The Judgement' and *The Metamorphosis*

'The Judgement'

The writing of 'The Judgement' ('Das Urteil') coincides with a turning point in Kafka's life. On 13 August 1912, he met his future fiancée Felice Bauer, who was visiting Prague from Berlin. On 20 September, Kafka sent his first letter to

Berlin, initiating what would become his most formative but also most conflicted relationship. Two days later, in the night of 22–3 September, Kafka wrote 'The Judgement', which is commonly regarded as his breakthrough, the first of his 'mature' writings. After reading the story to a group of family and friends, Kafka commented: 'There were tears in my eyes. The indubitability of the story was confirmed' (25 September 1912; *D* 214/*TB* 463). Even years later, the normally self-critical Kafka stood by this verdict.

'The Judgement' is one of Kafka's most unsettling texts. It tells the story of a father who suddenly accuses his adult son of disloyalty and betrayal and then sentences him to death by drowning – a verdict to which the son submits without hesitation. Family relations only hovered in the background of Kafka's early writings, but now, in the texts written in 1912–13, they take centre stage.

In this Kafka is not alone. The conflict between father and son is a prominent theme in modernist literature, particularly in German Expressionism, where fathers typically represent a tyrannical and outdated social order. In these texts, filial rebellion – even parricide – becomes a catalyst for social and political change. This plotline reflects the towering influence of Sigmund Freud and his famous theory of the 'Oedipus complex', itself modelled on Sophocles' tragedy *Oedipus Rex* (c. 429–425 BC), about the Greek king who unwittingly kills his father and marries his mother. Freud uses this ancient Greek tragedy as a blueprint for the psychological dynamics within the modern nuclear family where, as he argues, the young son's affection for his mother leads him to regard his father as a rival and enemy. After writing 'The Judgement', Kafka notes in his diary, 'thoughts about Freud, of course' (23 September 1912; *D* 213/*TB* 461). Yet 'The Judgement' also departs from Freud's theories in important ways. For a start, Kafka's family is incomplete, consisting of only a father and son, for the mother died two years ago. Most important, the story ends with the very reverse of parricide: an aged father asserting his absolute, lethal authority over his son.

On the face of it, Georg Bendemann is a model son. He is engaged to a wealthy young woman and has taken over the family business, vastly increasing its size and profit. At the beginning, we see him gazing out of the window, a pose familiar from the lonely bachelors in *Meditation*. But in Georg's case this pose spells not melancholy but contented reflection as he takes stock of his achievements. This reflection is prompted by a letter he has just written to a childhood friend who has moved to Russia to start a business. As a remnant of Georg's childhood, the friend is both familiar and alien. He represents a time, an identity, which Georg has had to leave behind in order to take on the father's role. Accordingly, Georg is torn between affection and distance. Should he advise his friend to give up his failing business and return home?

The first part of the story is thus rather uneventful, as it is mostly taken up with Georg's reflections about his friend. Like many of Kafka's texts, 'The Judgement' is a third-person narrative coloured by the protagonist's perspective and interpretation of events. This makes it difficult to judge how accurate Georg's image of his friend really is. The remainder of the narrative is made up largely of dialogue. Having finished the letter, Georg goes to see his father. What follows is an increasingly surreal conversation in which the friend once again plays a central role. The father, still in his dressing gown, is sitting in a room that has been turned into a shrine to the mother's memory. He shows all the signs of decrepitude, and yet when he gets up to greet his son, Georg cannot help thinking, 'my father is still a giant' (*M* 22/*DL* 50). From the start, then, the father is an ambiguous figure, combining strength and weakness. Compliantly, he lets Georg undress him, but as Georg carries him to bed like a baby, an apparent gulf opens up between appearance and reality: 'no sooner was he in bed than everything seemed fine'. The verb 'to seem' recurs again when the father asks Georg, '"Am I well covered over now?" . . . and seemed to pay particular attention to Georg's reply' (*M* 25/*DL* 55). Such formulations create a subtle sense of uncertainty and unease. When Georg replies, 'Quietly, now. You are well covered over' (*M* 25/*DL* 55), this reassuring remark sparks a dramatic change:

> 'No!' shouted the father, so sharply that the reply jolted against the question; he threw the bedspread back with such strength that for a moment it opened out completely in its flight, and stood upright in his bed. With only one hand he held lightly onto the ceiling. 'You wanted to cover me over, I know, my little sprig [*mein Früchtchen*], but I'm not covered over yet. And even if this is the last of my strength, it's enough for you, too much for you.'   (*M* 26/*DL* 56)

As Georg tries to reassure his father that he is well tucked up in bed, well 'covered over', the father discerns a more sinister intention behind this remark – namely Georg's desire to have him covered up (buried) for good. Conversely, the father derives his own newfound strength from his ability to *un*cover: his own, still powerful body, but also his son's intention of usurping his position in the business and the family.

Language becomes the site of their struggle. Initially, Georg seems to be in control of language when he writes to his friend, weighing up what he should or should not say. Thus he uses the engagement 'of some quite inconsequential person to some equally inconsequential girl' (*M* 21/*DL* 47) as a diversion from his own affairs, but by mentioning this event in three separate letters, he inadvertently arouses his friend's suspicion. Such 'Freudian slips' become more pronounced in the conversation with the father, who picks up on double meanings in his son's speech and reveals that he has been secretly writing to the friend, countering Georg's version of events. As he gleefully says, 'I wrote to him because you forgot to take my writing things away from me' (*M* 27/*DL* 59). Father and son are locked in a battle over written and spoken language, a battle from which the father emerges victorious. As Georg becomes increasingly silent, his replies confused and ineffectual, the father turns into a maliciously shrewd analyst, dissecting his son's every utterance for compromising hidden meanings.

The gulf between manifest and latent meaning, between appearance and reality, runs through the entire story. When his father calls himself the friend's representative, Georg impulsively calls out 'Comedian!' – only to immediately bite his lip. Again, the father is quick to pick up on this slip, declaring, 'Yes, of course I was acting a comedy! Comedy! A good word for it!' (*M* 27/*DL* 58). 'Comedy' and 'comedian' are key words in the story. The roles we play – whether in the family or at work – are not 'natural' but acquired over time. The father's comic performance is not funny but profoundly unsettling, as it turns life into a grotesque farce and turns him into a stranger to his son.

Pitted against this performative model, however, is another, more 'natural' conception of identity. Leaping on to his bed, the father calls Georg 'my little sprig' (in German *mein Früchtchen*, 'my little fruit'), and he builds on this image at the end of the story:

> How slow you were to mature! Your mother had to die. She didn't live to see the happy day. Your friend is going to ruin in his Russia – as long as three years ago he was yellow enough to throw away, and as for me – well, you can see how things are going with me. (*M* 28/*DL* 60)

The father uses organic metaphors of growth, ripening and decay to describe human life. In Georg's case, however, this natural cycle is cut short. Having grown up to take up his designated role in family and society, he will not be allowed to mature and grow old but will be 'harvested' in his prime. Most disturbingly, the father reveals that this lethal trajectory was set out from the start, and was, indeed, eagerly awaited by his mother, who died before it came to fruition.

The father's final pronouncement cements this sense of inevitability: 'After all, you were an innocent child really – but more really you were a diabolical human being! And therefore know: I condemn you now to death by drowning!' (*M* 28/*DL* 60). The father here rewrites his son's life story in a way which leaves no way out. Childhood innocence must turn into evil; indeed, the two are identical, and Georg, swept away by the logic of his argument, rushes out of the house to carry out the father's verdict. His dying moment highlights the bitter irony of Kafka's story: 'Dear parents, I did always love you', he calls 'softly', before letting himself drop into the water (*M* 28/*DL* 60). Georg's assertion can be read as a last protestation of innocence against his parents, who were unable to appreciate his love for them, and yet it is precisely this continued devotion that seals his fate. Ultimately, Kafka's sons are crushed and destroyed not by the power and aggression wielded by the fathers but by the emotional bond which ties them to their parents and which wipes out all resistance.

In the final sentence, the story pans away from Georg's suicide: 'At this moment there flowed over the bridge an absolutely unending stream of traffic' (*M* 28/*DL* 62). The German *Verkehr* is a key word in Kafka's texts. It means 'traffic', but also 'circulation' and 'exchange': of goods and money, letters, information and bodies.[3] In addition, *Verkehr* can also be translated as 'intercourse', and Kafka told his friend Max Brod that when he wrote the final sentence, he was thinking of an ejaculation. Georg's death is drowned out by the bustle of modern life, his demise overwritten by ongoing, (pro)creative activity. Here, as so often in Kafka's texts, the ending is also a new beginning. In fact, for Kafka 'The Judgement' sparked a flurry of creative activity. He entered into a feverish correspondence with Felice Bauer, and in the following months also wrote his first novel, *The Man who Disappeared*, and the novella *The Metamorphosis*.

This creative momentum also manifests itself as critical self-reflection. Kafka wrote 'The Judgement' in one night, and immediately after finishing it, he tried to describe this experience:

> The terrible strain and joy, how the story developed before me, as if I were advancing in water. Several times during this night I carried my own weight on my back. How everything can be dared, how for everything, for the strangest ideas, there waits a great fire in which they perish and rise up again ... Only in this way can writing be done, only with such coherence, with such a complete opening-out of the body and the soul. (23 September 1912; *D* 212–13/*TB* 460–1)

The writing process produces contrasting associations – joy and exhaustion, destruction and renewal, a sense of burden as well as of levitation. It is an experience both intimate and profoundly alien, which transgresses the boundaries of body and soul. This cathartic experience would occupy Kafka for months to come and became an integral part of his authorial self-image. In 1913, he writes: 'the story came out of me like a real birth, covered in filth and slime, and only I have the hand that can reach to the body itself and the desire to do so' (11 February 1913; *D* 214/*TB* 491). Here the metaphorical 'opening-out of the body' is transformed into an image of giving birth. The product is filthy and repellent, but its messiness forms part of Kafka's organic conception of writing. Even when working on longer projects, Kafka never produced a plan, and he rarely rewrote existing texts. Like an actual body, the text is an organic whole which does not lend itself to chopping and changing.

This approach has advantages but also severe drawbacks. As the notebooks show, the vast majority of Kafka's texts are unfinished, and many are abandoned after just one or two sentences. If a text is an organic whole, its core, its essence must be contained within the first sentence. If the beginning lacks this creative spark, no amount of hard work will be able to bring it to life. For Kafka, the ecstatic creation of 'The Judgement' becomes the benchmark for all future endeavours, but it turns out to be an elusive ideal. A few weeks later, in November 1912, he started work on *The Metamorphosis*. Here the notion of unity – whether physical, psychological or textual – is put to a severe test.

The Metamorphosis

The Metamorphosis is probably Kafka's most famous text. Written in November and December 1912, the story about salesman Gregor Samsa, who wakes up to find himself transformed into a giant insect, has become emblematic of the 'Kafkaesque': of a nightmarish situation which defies rational explanation. Like 'The Judgement', it is a story about family relations – about a conflict between father and son, but also between brother and sister. In many respects, however, *The Metamorphosis* is actually rather atypical of Kafka's writings. His texts often deal with strange and inexplicable situations, but they rarely break the conventions of realism so openly. One possible exception are Kafka's animal stories, whose protagonists possess human faculties of reason and language, but even here the essential boundary separating humans and animals remains intact. In *The Metamorphosis*, this boundary is crossed, making it Kafka's most fantastical story, a text which is often categorized as Expressionist. This label is accurate only in part. The text's premise may be fantastical, but its narrative tone points in a very different direction. One of the first things we are struck by when reading *The Metamorphosis* is the understated, calm and factual way in which Gregor's transformation is narrated. The narrative lacks any of the emotions – horror, shock, surprise – which we would associate with such a disturbing discovery.

This does not detract from the strangeness of the situation but makes it all the more disconcerting. Like Gregor Samsa, the man trapped inside an insect's body, Kafka's text is a strange hybrid. Stylistically it harks back to the conventions of nineteenth-century realism with its detailed, detached depiction of outside reality, but this is combined with an inward-looking psychological narration, which is the hallmark of literary modernism. Written in the third person, it is often coloured by Gregor's personal viewpoint, although intermittently an impersonal narrator comments on events. The distinction between these two narrative modes – the personal and the omniscient – is sometimes hard to draw.

The story's opening sentence is a case in point: 'As Gregor Samsa woke one morning from uneasy dreams, he found himself transformed into some kind of monstrous vermin' (*M* 29/*DL* 115) (see Fig. 3). By telling us that Gregor has just woken up, the text prevents us from dismissing what follows as a dream, and yet the reflexive verb 'found himself' lends this discovery a subjective, potentially unreliable, dimension. Has Gregor actually been transformed, or is this just a figment of his imagination? This mixture of certainty and uncertainty continues into the next paragraph: '"What has happened to me?" he thought. It was not a dream' (*M* 29/*DL* 115). First we are given a direct insight into Gregor's thoughts, but this is followed by an impersonal statement. Who is telling us that this is not a dream – Gregor, or an omniscient narrator? The following sentence seems relatively straightforward: 'His room, a proper, human being's room, rather too small, lay peacefully between its four familiar walls' (*M* 29/*DL* 115). But by spelling out the obvious – that rooms are inhabited by humans – the text reflects Gregor's growing distance from his old life, a process whereby the ordinary becomes strange and unsettling. In fact, although the room is here described as 'too small', Gregor will soon feel oppressed by its high ceilings and will seek refuge under the sofa.

Kafka's narrative, then, is full of subtle intricacies. Apparently straightforward formulations contain hidden depths and throw up unanswerable questions. This sense of uncertainty is nowhere more apparent than in relation to Gregor's body. In the first sentence we are told that Gregor has been turned into 'some kind of monstrous vermin'. The German 'ein ungeheueres Ungeziefer' is a double negative. The noun *Ungeziefer* originally referred to unclean animals which were unfit to be sacrificed; the adjective *ungeheuer*, 'monstrous' or 'enormous', is the negation of *geheuer*, 'familiar', but as in the case of *Ungeziefer*, the negative form is the more common. By using two words where the negative has become the main form, Kafka creates a vacuum of meaning. Faced with Gregor's transformation, language can only gesture towards something that resists explanation.

Throughout the text, the perspective on Gregor's body is unstable and fragmented. This is partially due to Gregor's limited perspective, which allows him to see only certain parts of his body, and partially due to the narrative itself. The text's sometimes pedantic attention to detail makes it hard for the reader to get a sense of the bigger picture. In the second part, we get a rare

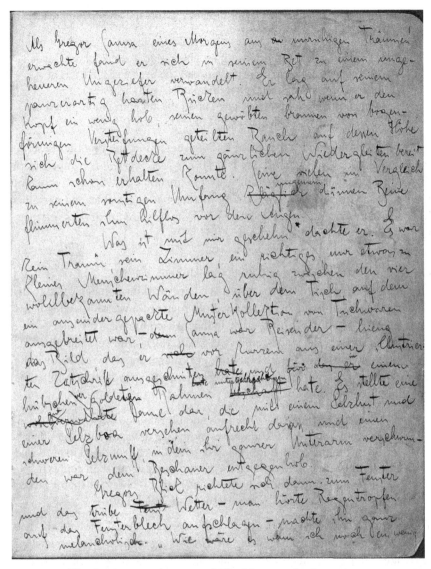

3 The first manuscript page of *The Metamorphosis*

outside view of Gregor as he clings to a picture on the wall, but all his startled mother can see is a 'giant brown patch on the flowered wallpaper' (*M* 56/*DL* 166). Like a horror filmmaker, Kafka creates suspense through omission, and when in 1915 *The Metamorphosis* was about to appear as a book, Kafka instructed the artist who was to draw the cover illustration to do the same. Rejecting the idea of depicting 'the insect' on the cover, he writes:

> If I were to offer suggestions for an illustration, I would choose such scenes as the following: the parents and the head clerk in front of the locked door, or even better, the parents and the sister in the lighted room, with the door open upon the adjoining room that lies in darkness.   (25 October 1915; *LFFE* 115/*DLA* 189–90)

The illustrator followed the gist of Kafka's suggestion, inviting the reader to imagine what lurks in the dark (see Fig. 4). *The Metamorphosis* compels us to fill in the blanks while preventing us from forming a definitive, coherent mental image. In this way, Gregor's monstrous body resembles the narrative itself – an ambivalent, unstable entity which has inspired countless interpretations but can be reduced to none.

Gregor's transformation: metaphor, punishment, release

Like Georg Bendemann, Gregor Samsa is a hard-working son dedicated to his career and the well-being of his family. Both men are successful – Gregor has risen from the position of a 'little clerk' to that of a 'commercial traveller' whose income can support the whole family (*M* 48/*DL* 152) – and yet their positions are very different. While Georg is about to get married and has taken over the family business, Gregor is lonely and dependent. He spends most of his time travelling because he has to pay off his parents' debt to his boss:

> 'Oh God!' he thought. 'What a strenuous profession I've chosen! Day in, day out on the move. The stresses of making deals are far greater than they are in the actual business at home. And on top of that, I'm burdened with the misery of travelling; there's the worry about train connections, the poor, irregular meals, human contact that is always changing, never lasting, never approaching warmth.'   (*M* 29/*DL* 116)

The unending traffic which drowned out Georg's death at the end of 'The Judgement' recurs at the beginning of *The Metamorphosis*. As a travelling salesman, Gregor is caught up in the soulless dynamism of modern life, where the circulation of money, goods and people has replaced meaningful human contact. The rat race of capitalism is a common theme in early-twentieth-century literature and film; Expressionist writers often tell stories of spiritual, as well as political, awakening, of people who break away from a soul-destroying routine into a new, more authentic form of existence. The title of Kafka's novella seems to point in a similar direction. In English, the text has become known as *(The) Metamorphosis*, a title which harks back to the

4 The cover of the first edition of *The Metamorphosis* (1916)

mythological tales of Ovid's *Metamorphoses*. However, a more accurate translation of *Die Verwandlung* is 'The Transformation'. This title points to another literary model: the fairy tale, where people are transformed into animals by an evil spell. Gregor Samsa's story harks back to this tradition, but also diverges from it in important ways. The reason behind his transformation is never explained, and the story ends not with the breaking of the spell, but with his death. Most importantly, to read Gregor's transformation as a punishment would be to simplify what is a much more complex issue.

In fact, Gregor's story raises one simple but tricky question: is this a change for the better or for the worse? On one level, Gregor's transformation is a continuation of his human existence. Gregor describes a colleague as 'the boss's creature, stupid and spineless' (*M* 31/*DL* 118), but this description also applies to himself. His new, 'spineless' body – that of an invertebrate – makes literal what has been the case metaphorically all along: a life of loneliness, subjugation and inhuman drudgery. This reading, however, does not resolve the contradictions inherent to Gregor's new state. The term 'vermin' (*Ungeziefer*) implies a parasitic existence, but up until now Gregor's family were the parasites, relying on him to fund their leisurely lifestyle. As a result, Gregor's transformation brings with it a great sense of liberation. Wedded to his gruelling routine, Gregor initially, absurdly, plans to catch the next train, but soon he settles into his new state and learns to control his animal body: 'He was particularly fond of hanging up under the ceiling. This was something different from lying on the floor; one breathed more freely; an easy swinging motion passed through the body' (*M* 52/*DL* 159). This levity corresponds to a new state of mind. Gregor's fixation on timetables and sales targets gives way to a state of 'almost happy ... distraction' (*M* 52/*DL* 159), and even when he accidentally lets go and crashes down on the floor, he does not injure himself. In this state of happy solitude, Gregor seems invincible, and it is only when he makes contact with his family that his body turns out to be vulnerable. In fact, Gregor's story is punctuated by a succession of progressively more serious, and eventually lethal, injuries.

Family narratives

Gregor's wounds are inflicted by his own family. Arguably, the true horror of *The Metamorphosis* lies not in Gregor's transformation but in his family's response. Once in each of the novella's three parts, Gregor ventures out of his room, and each time he is driven back. These confrontations are led by the father, although later they also involve his sister Grete, who initially acted as Gregor's carer. Indeed, the title of the novella applies as much to the family as to Gregor himself. The changes they undergo are less sudden but no less disconcerting. His mother and sister take up paid work, Grete maturing from a schoolgirl to a young woman whose neck is on show, 'free of ribbon or collar' (*M* 67/*DL* 186).

Herr Samsa's transformation is the most radical. When he returns home one day, Gregor barely recognizes him. He who used to spend the entire day dozing in his armchair is now dressed in 'a tight blue uniform with gold buttons' (*M* 58/*DL* 169), and this trim outfit is matched by his upright posture and penetrating gaze. Like Herr Bendemann, Herr Samsa has turned from a decrepit old man into a towering giant; gazing up at him, 'Gregor was amazed at the gigantic size of his boot-soles' (*M* 58/*DL* 170). A photograph in the living room shows Gregor as a lieutenant during his military service, 'with his hand on his sword, smiling light-heartedly, demanding respect for his posture and uniform' (*M* 39/*DL* 135). Now the father seems to have morphed into his son, emulating his earlier pose of strength and confidence. Of course, the father is not a soldier but merely a bank servant, but he is so wedded to his new role that he refuses to take off his uniform even at home; when he falls asleep in it in his armchair, he looks 'as if he were always ready for duty and waiting here too for the voice of his superior' (*M* 60/*DL* 173).

Once he has recovered from his initial shock, Gregor notices that although the buttons on his father's uniform are shiny, the fabric is covered in stains. In this, the father resembles Herr Bendemann, whose dressing gown falls open to reveal his dirty underwear. In both cases, dirt becomes a shorthand for weakness and neglect – but also for the seeping-through of unsavoury urges. Herr Bendemann lifts up his nightshirt, insinuating that Georg's fiancée might have done the same to seduce his son. In *The Metamorphosis*, sexuality erupts into ordinary family life in an equally shocking manner. The text's dramatic climax occurs towards the end of the second part, when Gregor, having emerged from his room, is pelted by his father with apples. As he is hit, Gregor feels as if he is being 'nailed fast' on the floor (*M* 59/*DL* 171). This image has religious overtones, casting Gregor as a modern-day Christ, the innocent victim of his family's aggression, but also sexual ones – the penetration of the emasculated vermin-son by the all-powerful phallic father.

Soon the sexual overtones become more explicit. The mother emerges from Gregor's bedroom, 'in her shift, for his sister had undressed her so that she could breathe more easily during her faint', and, dropping her underskirts on the way, she 'stumbled over the skirts to urge herself upon their father, embracing him, in total union with him – Gregor's sight was already failing – and with her hands circling the back of his father's head she begged him to spare Gregor's life' (*M* 59/*DL* 171). Freud coined the term 'primal scene' to describe a child's (real or imagined) witnessing of his/her parents' intercourse – an experience that can have a traumatic effect on the young observer. Gregor is no child, and yet at this moment his eyes fail him, as if to shield him from this disturbing sight. For once it is the mother who plays the active part, as she embraces the father to the point of their 'total union'. This is designed to save Gregor from his father's wrath, but the scene also emphasizes the unity of the parents, as well as their renewed sexual prowess, which sharply contrasts with Gregor's isolated, disempowered position.

That said, Gregor himself is not without sexual urges. One of the first things he notices when he wakes up are small white spots on his belly – the residue of 'nocturnal emissions' brought on by his uneasy dreams? Having examined his new body, Gregor's gaze is drawn to a picture on the wall opposite, which he has cut out from a magazine and put into a homemade gilded frame. This image shows a woman clad in fur, but its description is sketchy and rather allusive. Is it a fashion photograph, or an erotic, even pornographic image? Since only her fur hat, muff and stole are described, critics have speculated that the sitter might be naked underneath. Fur has animalistic, sexual – pubic – overtones, but as with the white spots on Gregor's belly, such formulations remain ambiguous, open to any number of readings and associations. One possible allusion here is to Leopold von Sacher-Masoch's erotic novel *Venus in Furs* (1896). Its protagonist, Severin, adopts the name Gregor when he enslaves himself to the Russian countess Wanda, who embodies his fetishistic idol, the eponymous Venus in Furs. With her upright posture and raised arm, the woman in Gregor Samsa's picture is latently threatening, a dominatrix to match Gregor's own masochistic tendencies. When Grete and the mother try to clear out his room, however, his submissiveness turns into aggression. Gregor defiantly crawls on to the picture to stop them from taking it. The picture, which depicts a kind of human–animal hybrid, is a monstrosity in its own right. The scene in which Gregor presses his hot belly against the cool glass is latently comical as well as grotesque. By choosing to save this picture rather than, say, his desk, Gregor clings to the animalistic side of his past, and yet the picture in its homemade gilded frame represents a tamed, domesticated version of such 'savage' desires.

Music, death and new beginnings

Gilles Deleuze and Félix Guattari describe Gregor's story as a process of 'becoming-animal' – a gradual, liberating journey away from the confines of human identity.[4] But this is not a linear process. Time and again, the father asserts his power over Gregor, and Gregor himself remains torn between embracing his animality and hanging on to his human self. His attitude towards his family is mostly gentle and forgiving, his behaviour timid and submissive. When he does rebel, this rebellion is driven by desire. His defence of the gilt-framed picture is one such moment; another occurs towards the end of the novella.

The three lodgers who move into the family flat in the third part are unnerving figures. They move and act as one, like puppets or automata. During dinner, they do not speak but read the newspaper; all Gregor hears from inside his room is the grinding of their teeth. As he thinks to himself, 'How these gentlemen feed themselves, and I perish' (*M* 65/*DL* 183). But the three also rival Gregor with regard to other appetites. Grete's violin-playing, which used to provide a special bond between her and Gregor, is offered up to the lodgers as entertainment. During the recital, they stand 'much too close behind the sister's music-stand' (*M* 66/*DL* 185), and although they soon lose interest, their presence has a strange effect on Gregor. Attracted by Grete's playing, he ventures into the living room, trying to catch her gaze: 'Was he a beast, that music should move him like this? He felt as if the way to the unknown nourishment he longed for was being revealed' (*M* 66/*DL* 185). Gregor's animal nature may seem incompatible with a taste for music, but in fact the opposite is the case. He had to leave behind his alienated human existence to learn to appreciate other, higher things. Music, the text suggests, is nourishment for the soul rather than the body, although Grete's playing also triggers distinctly sexual cravings in her brother:

> He resolved to advance right up to his sister, pluck her by the skirt to intimate that he was asking her to come with her violin into his room, for no one here was rewarding her playing as he would reward it. He wouldn't let her out of his room ever again, at least not while he was alive; his terrifying figure should be useful to him for the first time; he would post himself by all the doors of his room at once and go hissing to meet his attackers; but his sister should stay with him, not under duress, but of her own free will; she should sit next to him on the sofa, incline her ear down to him, and he would confide to her his firm intention of sending her to the conservatoire ... After this explanation his sister would burst into tears of emotion and Gregor would rear up as far as her shoulders and kiss her throat, which, ever since she had been working at the shop, was free of ribbon or collar. (*M* 67/*DL* 185–6)

This scene recalls fairy tales such as 'Beauty and the Beast', but in this version the love of an innocent maiden does not lift the spell – and for good reasons. Gregor's animality is an integral part of this erotic fantasy. Not only does it enable him to scare away intruders, but when he imagines kissing Grete (rather than she him, as is customary in such cases), he does so as an animal, raising himself up from below. Here Kafka abandons Freud's Oedipal model in favour of a different form of desire. Gregor's erotic fairy tale unites two of the most transgressive perversions: incest and bestiality, endogamy and extreme exogamy. The bourgeois family, Kafka's novella suggests, is a breeding ground for all kinds of perversions, and Gregor Samsa's transformation from model son to monster exposes what has been lurking beneath the surface all along.

This is why the Samsas are so keen to exclude Gregor from their midst, but the harder they try the more their own inhumanity is revealed. During their first encounter, the father 'hiss[es] like a savage' (*M* 42/*DL* 140), and any minute Gregor expects him to deal him the fatal blow. This fatal blow does come, belatedly, in the form of the apple which is lodged in Gregor's back, but in the end it is the sister who pronounces the death sentence. 'It has to go', she declares after Gregor's encounter with the lodgers (*M* 69/*DL* 191). Although Grete has not spoken directly to Gregor, her announcement amounts to a death sentence similar to that pronounced by Herr Bendemann in 'The Judgement'. Gregor retreats to his room to die: 'His last glance fell on his mother, who by now had fallen fast asleep' (*M* 70/*DL* 192).

'Dear parents, I always loved you' (*M* 28/*DL* 61), Georg Bendemann calls out as he jumps off the bridge, and Gregor dies with similar sentiments:

> He thought back on his family with affection and love. His own opinion that he should vanish was, if possible, even more determined than his sister's. He remained in this state of vacant and peaceful reflection until the tower clock struck three in the morning. He still lived to see the dark begin to grow generally lighter outside the window. Then his head sank down without his willing it, and from his nostrils his last breath faintly flowed.   (*M* 71/*DL* 193–4)

Here, a more emotional tone enters the sober narrative, and even Kafka himself is moved. As he writes to Felice Bauer: 'Cry, dearest, cry, the time for crying has come! The hero of my little story died a while ago. To comfort you, I want you to know that he died peacefully enough and reconciled to all' (5/6 December 1912; *LF* 112/*BF* 160). Yet the text does not end on this cathartic note. Our tears dry up as we observe the aftermath of Gregor's death, the account of his family's response, which is narrated in a more detached tone.

Kafka disliked the ending, calling it 'imperfect almost to its very marrow' (19 January 1914; D 253/*TB* 624), probably because it disrupted the organic unity of the text. Gregor's death brings about a shift of narrative perspective. The father and mother become 'Herr and Frau Samsa', and the narrative focus is no longer tied to Gregor but shifts between characters and locations. Thus we follow the charwoman into Gregor's room as she discovers his body and again as she shows it to the three lodgers; although we are told that the three Samsas emerge from the parents' bedroom 'show[ing] signs of weeping' (*M* 72/*DL* 196), we actually witness only their more composed behaviour in response to Gregor's death. Looking at his flat and dried-out body, Grete comments: 'Just see how thin he was. He hasn't eaten now for so long' (*M* 72/*DL* 195). It is only after his death that the family can refer to him as 'he' again, whereas beforehand Grete had taken to calling him 'this beast' (*M* 69/*DL* 191).

The ending is a kind of epilogue. The Samsas have regained their humanity, and a new sense of purpose. Together with Gregor's emaciated corpse, other foreign elements are expelled from the family space. Herr Samsa throws out the lodgers and announces that the charwoman will be dismissed that night. To celebrate their new-found freedom, the Samsas escape from the prison of their flat and take the tram to the countryside. Their arrival marks a new departure. Noticing how Grete has blossomed into 'a handsome, full-figured girl' (*M* 74/ *DL* 200), her parents silently agree that she should soon be introduced to the marriage market. The family narrative continues despite the death of its protagonist. Both 'The Judgement' and *The Metamorphosis* start slowly, almost hesitantly, but by the end both texts have gained enough momentum to point beyond their own conclusion towards other, ongoing stories.

The Man who Disappeared

The roots of Kafka's first novel, *The Man who Disappeared* (*Der Verschollene*, also known as *Amerika*), go back a long way. As early as 1898–9, Kafka planned to write a novel about two feuding brothers, one of whom travels to America while the other is locked up in a European prison. Over a decade later, he returned to this project, but now the two storylines of punishment and emigration are combined in the figure of seventeen-year-old Karl Rossmann, who is sent to America as a punishment for sexual misconduct. Kafka worked on a first draft between December 1911 and July 1912, but this version has not survived. In September 1912, fired up by the success of 'The Judgement', he made a fresh start and quickly completed five chapters. In November, he interrupted work on the novel to write *The Metamorphosis*, but when he returned to it he found it difficult to get back into the flow and stopped working on the novel in January 1913. But Kafka was not ready to give up on the project just yet. In the autumn of 1914, while working on *The Trial*, he returned to *The Man who Disappeared* once more with a new storyline, which describes Karl's entry into the mysterious 'Oklahama Theatre' (Kafka's spelling). Despite Kafka's renewed effort to complete *The Man who Disappeared*, however, it ultimately remained unfinished – a fate it shares with his other novels, *The Trial* and *The Castle*.

'Film screening at the Landestheater. Box seat. Fräulein Oplatka, who was once pursued by a clergyman. She arrived home completely drenched in a cold sweat. Danzig. Körner's Life. The horses. The white horse. The smoke of gunpowder. Lützow's wild chase' (D 214/*TB* 463). So ends Kafka's diary entry of 25 September 1912. After a horizontal line, he begins the first chapter of *The Man who Disappeared.* Work on the novel is thus immediately preceded by an account of a cinema visit, an experience which, before the advent of the feature film, would have consisted of several short pieces. Kafka only sketches out a few scenes, conveying a sense of dynamism. Horses and gunpowder smoke accompany Lützow on his 'wild chase', while poor Fräulein Oplatka is chased by a clergyman, a storyline which suggests a comedy or farce but which Kafka gives a more sinister dimension by singling out the girl's 'cold sweat'. Excitement and exhilaration are tinged with fear, a tension which also underpins the novel.

   The Man who Disappeared is the most readable of Kafka's novels, for the format of the travelogue allows for a quick change of location and atmosphere, resulting in a narrative which is pacier than Kafka's two subsequent novels. The text paints a colourful panorama of America in the early twentieth century, from the skyscrapers of New York City to the vast expanse of the Midwest, and on his travels Karl Rossmann meets people from all walks of life. As we have seen, Kafka's fascination with the United States is evident from his earliest texts. Red Indians feature in several of the pieces of *Meditation*, most notably in 'Wish to Become a Red Indian', where the ride across the steppes turns into the movement of the pen across the blank page. The New World and its inhabitants become the vehicle for Kafka's literary ambition, and he tries to carry over this momentum into his first novel, a big task which requires all the energy he can muster.

   No Red Indians feature in *The Man who Disappeared*, which describes the New World not through American eyes – as a natural space of boundless freedom – but from the perspective of a European emigrant. The image that emerges is far from positive. Karl's journey through the United States is really an odyssey, punctuated by experiences of punishment and betrayal. Kafka's America is populated by characters who are deceitful, exploitative, or just plain sadistic. But this is only one side of the story. Walter Benjamin calls Karl the 'happier incarnation of K., the hero of Kafka's novels';[5] indeed, Karl's many disappointments are counterbalanced by almost miraculous opportunities. As the narrative wears on, however, we come to recognize this pattern and anxiously await the next disappointment, each more bitter than the last. On the whole, the narrative follows a downward spiral, tracing Karl's descent from the heights of American society to its very bottom, and its lighter, happier moments cast the surrounding darkness into greater relief.

Beginnings: 'The Stoker'

Kafka's novel opens with the Statue of Liberty, that most iconic of American landmarks. This sight, however, is given a twist, indicating to the reader that this is no conventional travelogue:

> As the seventeen-year-old Karl Rossmann, who had been sent to America by his poor parents because a servant-girl had seduced him and had a child by him, entered New York harbour in the already slowing ship, he saw the statue of the Goddess of Liberty, which he had been observing for some time, as though in a sudden blaze of sunlight. Her arm with the sword stretched upward as though newly raised and the free breezes wafted around her.   (*MD* 5/*V* 7)

In one long opening sentence Kafka sums up the protagonist's past and present, but this account is not without ambiguity. By referring to Karl's 'poor parents', the text implies sympathy with their plight, when in fact it is Karl who deserves our sympathy. Karl's is a story of harsh and unjust punishment, and his first impression of America does not bode well for the future. The Statue of Liberty is a symbol of freedom and enlightenment, but in Kafka's novel it takes on a more threatening dimension. The torch carried by the real Statue is here transformed into a sword, and the Statue is described as a 'Goddess'. The 'free breezes' thus surround a figure of supernatural authority – or so it seems to Karl. Twice in this opening section Kafka uses the formulation 'as though', lending the scene a highly subjective dimension. As the ship enters the harbour, the statue seems lit up '*as though* in a sudden blaze of sunlight'. This moment is typical of the novel as a whole. Time and again, continuous perception gives way to moments of heightened alertness, whereby the dynamism of modern life is arrested in quasi-photographic tableaux. 'So high', Karl thinks to himself as he looks up at the Statue (*MD* 5/*V* 7). Like Georg Bendemann and Gregor Samsa, he is confronted by a towering figure of authority which makes him feel small and insignif-icant, but this time the figure is female – an important detail which sets the tone for the rest of the novel. Kafka's text is full of powerful women who use sexuality as a tool of domination.

Although the Statue marks the ship's arrival in the United States, Karl does not set foot on American soil until much later. Just as he is about to disembark, he suddenly remembers that he has forgotten his umbrella. To fetch it, he leaves behind an even more precious possession: his suitcase, which he had anxiously guarded on his journey. Throughout the novel inanimate objects lead a curious life of their own. Karl's few possessions – his umbrella and the suitcase containing, among other things, a photograph of his parents – are the last tangible links to his past. These objects are caught up in a pattern of disappearance and reappearance, until eventually they are lost for good. Karl's possessions stand for a past which is slipping away from him, but they also reflect his own, deeply ambivalent stance towards his origins. As Freud argued in his *Psychopathology of Everyday Life* (1901), nothing we do is accidental, least of all slips and oversights, which in fact betray hidden, disavowed motivations. As Karl tells Herr Green, his suitcase is in fact 'my father's old army suitcase' (*MD* 63/*V* 124). The suitcase is an heirloom, part of a cherished tradition – in New York Karl likes to play 'one of the old military songs from his home' (*MD* 32/*V* 60) on the piano – but it is also a burden. Karl's attachment to his European things goes hand in hand with an unconscious desire to abandon the baggage of his traumatic past.

If Karl's possessions have a tendency to get lost, the same applies to their owner. Karl's hunt for his umbrella leads him back into the bowels of the ship, where he finds his usual route blocked and gets lost – the first of many such incidents. The ship is at once vast and claustrophobic, the first in a succession of labyrinthine spaces in the novel. Some of them, like the uncle's factory and the Hotel Occidental, are teeming with people; Herr Pollunder's country villa, in contrast, is dark, silent and empty. Its endless corridors, lined with rows of locked doors, lead Karl to a large, echoing chapel – a scene which anticipates Josef K.'s equally disorienting visit to the cathedral in *The Trial*. Such spaces reflect the protagonist's lack of direction; with his flickering candle, Karl resembles a sleepwalker trapped in a bad dream.

When the novel was published posthumously in 1927, it appeared under the title *Amerika*, which was chosen by Kafka's friend and editor Max Brod. Kafka himself used a different title: *Der Verschollene* ('the man who disappeared'). This title is peculiar even in German, and difficult to translate. It presumably refers to Karl, but in which sense, and from whose perspective, is Karl the 'man who disappeared'? As readers we follow his every step, but we quickly realize that Karl's journey lacks a sense of direction. He does not follow a fixed route but drifts further and further into the unknown, a stranger to others and to himself. In fact, Karl's story is less a travelogue than a story of exile – a parable of the modern subject who is fundamentally, existentially, uprooted. The nineteenth century saw a great increase in geographical and social mobility as people moved to the cities or even to foreign countries in search of a better life. Karl Rossmann embodies these aspirations; he too hopes for success and recognition, but these hopes are crushed time and again.

The Man who Disappeared has been compared to the *Bildungsroman*, or 'novel of formation', a narrative genre which traces the development of a young person into a mature and rounded individual. Karl's youth fits this model, but his experience does not. He is a strangely passive, 'flat' character, who seems incapable of strong emotions and does not learn from his many setbacks. The principle of his journey is not development but circularity, repetition and (psychological) regression.

The novel's beginning is a case in point. Rather than stepping off the ship and into his new life, Karl ends up back in the bowels of the ship, curled up on the stoker's bed. The stoker, 'a huge man' (*MD* 6/*V* 8), is the first in a series of mentors who take Karl under their wing. He is a father substitute, but also an ally, a fellow German in whom Karl recognizes his own situation. One of the things they have in common is a suspicion of 'foreigners'. The stoker feels oppressed by the Romanian chief engineer, Schubal, who 'treats us Germans on a German ship like dirt' (*MD* 8/*V* 13), and Karl, despite his youth, shares his prejudices. On the ship he hardly dared to sleep for fear that the 'little Slovak' (*MD* 9/*V* 16) sharing his cabin might steal his suitcase – but when he goes back to fetch his umbrella he entrusts his suitcase to a near-stranger, the Germanically named Franz Butterbaum. In the Habsburg Empire of Kafka's time, the Slavic peoples were ruled by a German-speaking elite, but this 'natural' hierarchy is reversed on the ship and even more so in the New World. As Karl complains to the stoker: 'Altogether, people here are so prejudiced against foreigners, I believe' (*MD* 8/*V* 13). This prejudice, based on no actual experience, nonetheless contains a kernel of truth. As he travels from Europe to America, Karl loses his place in a hierarchy based on class and ethnicity. While he continues to class others as 'foreigners', this barely masks the fact that he has himself become a stranger in a strange land.

In this situation, Karl's friendship with the stoker provides some sense of stability, but this friendship does not last. When a man in the captain's office turns out to be Karl's wealthy Uncle Jakob, Karl leaves the ship and his friend behind, and as they are rowed to the shore, it seems to Karl 'as though the stoker no longer existed' (*MD* 28/*V* 53). For Karl, then, the stoker is the 'man who disappeared'. Faced with this realization, Karl scrutinizes his uncle, 'and began to doubt whether this man could ever replace the stoker for him' (*MD* 28/*V* 53) – but this is precisely what will happen. In fact, substitution is one of the novel's core principles. Each time Karl is uprooted or expelled, one mentor is replaced by another, but once a personal tie is cut, it is as if it never existed. Karl rarely thinks back to previous encounters, and the narrator seems equally forgetful; thus only a handful of characters – the tricksters Robinson and Delamarche and the liftboy Giacomo – appear in more than one part of the novel. Whether he is dealing with objects or with people, Karl cannot form lasting attachments – a survival mechanism which enables him to keep moving forward, but which also spells inner stagnation. Starting afresh after each disappointment, Karl does not grow or evolve but merely repeats the same mistakes time and again.

The Man who Disappeared remained unfinished, but Kafka decided to publish the first chapter 'The Stoker' ('Der Heizer') as a self-contained text. In 1913, it appeared in the series *Der jüngste Tag* (*Judgement Day*), a forum for new Expressionist writing. 'The Stoker', then, is both an opening chapter and a self-contained story, and yet it has neither a real beginning nor a proper conclusion. True to the travelogue genre, it describes the protagonist's arrival in a new place, but then the narrative momentum peters out, and by the end Karl still has not set foot on American soil. His uncle, sitting opposite him in the rowing boat, avoids Karl's gaze and looks instead 'at the waves that were rising and falling around their boat' (*MD* 28/*V* 53). Personal connections are withdrawn almost as soon as they are established. At the end of 'The Stoker', Karl embarks on another journey into the unknown, in a scene full of foreboding.

Kafka's America: crowds and capitalism

Kafka never actually travelled to the United States. For information about the country he drew on various fictional and non-fictional sources, including novels, travelogues, lectures and slide shows. Several of Kafka's relatives had emigrated to the United States, and anecdotes and postcards detailing their experiences circulated within the family. But *The Man who Disappeared* also reflects Kafka's own travel experiences in Europe, in particular his trips to Paris in 1910 and 1911, where he witnessed a more fast-paced urban life. Just as Karl's experiences in the United States are shot through with memories of his European past, Kafka's America is a literary collage, an amalgam of life in the New World and the Old.

Here, as in other Kafka texts, one key word is traffic, *Verkehr*. Kafka's America is animated by constant hectic motion, by a perpetual stream of people and objects. From the balcony in his uncle's house, Karl observes the traffic in the streets below, which carries on 'from morning to evening and amid the dreams of the night' (*MD* 29/*V* 55). This traffic is not restricted to the outside world, but invades the mind – the realm of dreams, of the unconscious. Kafka's primary aim in *The Man who Disappeared* is not realist representation but a psychological exploration of the ways in which modernity conditions – disfigures – body and mind.

The company owned by Karl's Uncle Jakob, 'a kind of commission and delivery service' (*MD* 34/*V* 55), does not actually produce anything but merely manages the circulation of goods and information. Its nodal point is the telephone room. Here Karl gets to observe a telephone operator, his head encased in a steel band that pressed the earpieces against his ears. His right arm was lying on a small table as though it were particularly heavy, and only his fingers, holding the pencil, twitched with inhuman regularity and rapidity. The words he spoke into the speaking-tube were very economical and you could often see that he wanted to criticize something the speaker had said or question him more closely, but certain words he heard compelled him, before he could carry out his intention, to lower his eyes and write.   (*MD* 35/*V* 66–7)

The man's body is fused with the machine he operates; indeed, he has himself become like a machine, executing his repetitive tasks with superhuman speed and accuracy. Although he is on the phone, his job does not involve actual conversation. Modern technology obstructs human contact rather than enabling it. Indeed, Kafka himself was deeply suspicious of telephones, which in his texts often stand for a breakdown in communication.

The telephone operator embodies a capitalist ideal of alertness, of mind and body trained to levels of maximum efficiency. The psychological effects of modern working conditions have been summed up by the sociologist Max Horkheimer. As he argues, the modern worker is

> without dream or history, he is always watchful and ready, always aiming at some immediate practical goal ... He takes the spoken word only as a medium of information, orientation, and command ... The individual no longer has any future to care for, he has only to be ready to adapt himself, to follow orders, to pull levers, to perform ever different things which are ever the same.[6]

If all attention is focused on the task at hand, there is no scope for pause and reflection, no time to step out of the present and to reflect on the wider context. Initially, Karl only observes this situation from the outside, but at his next workplace he gets himself sucked into the capitalist machinery. As its name implies, the Hotel Occidental is the embodiment of Western capitalism. With its numerous elevators, entrances and side entrances, it is a self-contained universe, but also a slightly unreal, transitory place. The two porters in the lobby are besieged by guests and offer 'information without the slightest interruption' (*MD* 130/*V* 256). Karl's own work is highly pressured, and yet he eagerly throws himself into his post as a liftboy and soon outperforms the other boys.

Karl, then, has internalized the American dream, the hope of rising from 'rags to riches', and even when he becomes the servant of the tyrannical Brunelda he eagerly applies himself to his menial tasks, resolved to stick it out in the hope of finding a better position. Karl's ambitions are modest but revealing. He dreams that one day he might be 'an office worker sitting at his desk and gazing for a while, free from worries, through the open window' (*MD* 180/*V* 353). An office job might not be exciting – Kafka himself complained about his almost incessantly – but unlike the work of a liftboy it offers occasional scope for reverie, a momentary respite from the rat-race of capitalism. This, however, remains a dream. In reality, Karl never really has time to pause and reflect, either about himself or about society.

Despite that, *The Man who Disappeared* is Kafka's most explicitly political novel. It features strikes, election campaigns and demonstrations, although these scenes happen at a distance, out of Karl's reach. On their car journey to Herr Pollunder's villa, Karl and his host pass a demonstration of striking metalworkers that is taking place in the outskirts of New York (*MD* 39/*V* 74–5). From a distance, the crowd of demonstrators seems strangely controlled; they move as one, with 'tiny steps', and their chant is 'in unison greater than that of a single voice'. Here, uniformity and machine-like precision, which characterize all areas of capitalist labour, even extend to political protest. Conformity with the system and rebellion against it take the same outward form. Apart from this slowly moving crowd, however, the scene is eerily still, arrested as if by the flash of a camera. An empty tram carriage stands abandoned, and here and there a policeman surveys the scene 'on a motionless horse'. To Karl, the demonstration appears as a series of disjointed stills, a perspective which reflects his lack of inner involvement. Indeed, for most of the journey he does not even look out of the window but leans back 'happily in the arm that Mr Pollunder had put round him, the certainty that he would soon be a welcome guest in a well-lit country house surrounded by walls and guarded by dogs gave him an enormous sense of well-being'. In contrast to the first chapter, when he supported the stoker in his campaign for justice, Karl seems here to feel no solidarity with the striking workers, but only a desire for safety and shelter. The last scene he takes in from the car mirrors his inner distance: 'Small groups of inquisitive people were standing a long way from the real demonstrators, not moving from the spot although they were not sure what was actually happening.'

Later in the novel, Karl comes across another example of political action, but this time his response is very different. As Brunelda's servant, he only gets to see the outside world from her balcony. When an election campaign for the position of judge takes place in the street below, Karl has a good overview but is, once again, removed from the action. From where he stands, the placards appear blank, and he cannot understand the name of the candidate that is being chanted by the crowds. Kafka strips the ensuing debate of its content and focuses solely on its quality as a spectacle. Like the metal workers' demonstration, events seem carefully choreographed, but soon uniformity gives way to chaos: 'the crowd was drifting without a plan, one person was leaning on the next, nobody could stand upright any more' (*MD* 169/*V* 333). When the spotlights illuminating the scene are smashed up, aural impressions take over from visual ones: 'the deceptive effect of the darkness was further increased by the sudden beginning of a broad, uniform chanting that was approaching from the lower end, from the bridge' (*MD* 170/*V* 334).

As Karl is later told by the student, the candidate in question never really stood a chance, despite his crowd of supporters. Political action in Kafka's novel is little more than an empty spectacle. In the early twentieth century, when much of Europe was still under monarchical rule, the United States were a beacon of freedom and democracy, but *The Man who Disappeared* paints a more critical picture – of a society where protest is indistinguishable from conformity, and where true power structures are apparent only to the initiated.

Masculinity in crisis: gender, sexuality, desire

Among many social changes, the early twentieth century saw a struggle for female equality. After centuries of life tied to the home, women joined the workforce in large numbers and became more visible in public life. This was accompanied by better access to education and greater political participation, by sexual liberalization and a changing body image. Corsets and long dresses were replaced by lighter clothing, which allowed more space for movement and even physical exercise. Herr Pollunder's daughter Klara is a typical example of this so-called 'new woman'. She lifts Karl off his feet 'with her sport-toughened body' and tackles him with 'some exotic combat technique' before pinning him down on the sofa; Karl does not take kindly to this: 'You cat, you crazy cat', he exclaims with a mixture of 'fury and shame' (*MD* 47/*V* 90–1). He is not alone in this response, for women's emancipation provoked a misogynist backlash. In his pseudo-scientific treatise, *Sex and Character* (1903), the Austrian Otto Weininger argued that Woman was passive, illogical and amoral, a corrupting force that pulled Man down from the lofty heights of reason into the boggy terrain of desire. Weininger tried to essentialize the differences between men and women, giving them a scientific basis; his bestseller is symptomatic of a profound unease about gender roles in a state of flux.

This unease is reflected, as well as refracted, in Kafka's novel. During the stoker's negotiations, a sailor knocks on the captain's door and is about to salute when he exclaims: 'That's disgusting, they tied a girl's apron round my waist' (*MD* 27/*V* 50). The blurring of gender roles is neither funny nor liberating; indeed, in his visceral response the sailor is not alone. When

Karl is seduced by the thirty-five-year-old maidservant Johanna Brummer, he feels disgust rather than pleasure – or at least so it seems to him in hindsight. He recalls how the older woman 'fumbled with her hand between his legs in such a disgusting manner that Karl wriggled his head and neck out of the pillows' and then when she 'thrust her belly against him several times, he felt as though she were part of himself and perhaps for this reason he was seized by a terrible sense of needing help' (*MD* 23/*V* 43). Karl might simply lack the appropriate vocabulary, as well as the necessary experience, to recognize pleasure for what it is, but there is another way of interpreting his repulsion, namely as a response to the reversal of gender roles. In this sex scene, Karl is not thrusting and masculine but entirely passive. His account contains no mention of genitals but only a vague reference to the area 'between his legs'. To himself, Karl appears asexual, castrated, and his behaviour is more reminiscent of a child than of a man. Johanna in turn appears more like a mother than a lover; she undresses him and lays him on her bed 'as though she would henceforth entrust him to no one else and would caress and tend him until the end of the world' (*MD* 23/*V* 42).

Karl's account of his seduction is a virtuosic piece of narration, precariously balanced between knowledge and denial. Of course, one small but important detail that contradicts his desexualized version of events is the baby who is born as a result. This child is mentioned only twice in the novel: once in the first sentence and then again by Karl's uncle, who recounts receiving a letter from Johanna Brummer in which she tells him about the baby, a boy named Jakob. Here the child's story ends before it has properly begun. In a sense, the baby is the novel's first 'man who disappeared', and while his birth is central to Karl's story, his absence from the ensuing narrative is just as revealing. Karl is expelled by his parents, but by going to America he also eschews his own parental responsibilities – perhaps in an attempt to avoid emulating his parents' example. Given the track record of fathers in Kafka's fiction, this move is hardly surprising, and yet as a result Karl is neither son nor father, neither child nor man, but remains stuck somewhere in between the two.

This in-between state is apparent throughout the novel. When Klara tries to overpower him, Karl tears himself away only to embrace her in return:

> 'Oh you're hurting me,' she said at once. But now Karl thought he couldn't let her go ... Besides, it was so easy to keep his arms round her in her tight-fitting dress. 'Let me go,' she whispered, her flushed face close to his, it was an effort for him to see her, she was so close, 'let me go, I'll give you something nice.' 'Why is she sighing like that,' thought Karl, 'it can't hurt her, I'm not squeezing her,' and he still did not let her go. (*MD* 47/*V* 90)

The Man who Disappeared is full of scenes like this. Karl attracts the sexual appetites of both men and women, but even when he feels the stirrings of desire, he tries to maintain a childlike perspective, ignoring sexuality in others and in himself. The narrative mirrors this process of repression in passages which reveal what they simultaneously conceal.

This is particularly noticeable in cases of homoerotic desire. Like Johanna Brummer and Klara, the stoker pushes Karl onto his bed, but this time Karl does not seem to mind, and when they part, he kisses and caresses the stoker's hand and sheds bitter tears. 'The stoker seems to have cast a spell on you', his uncle comments, 'casting a knowing glance over Karl's head towards the Captain', but then he warns, 'But for my sake, don't take it too far' (*MD* 27/ *V* 50). The uncle's words and speaking glance resemble Kafka's own, equally allusive narrative strategy. When Herr Pollunder 'put his arm round Karl and drew him closer, between his legs' (*MD* 54/*V* 104), Karl is happy to give in to this 'paternal' embrace, stubbornly filtering out any sexual overtones. In relation to the sadistic head porter, this strategy is more difficult to uphold. Having cornered Karl, he declares: 'But now you're here, I'm going to enjoy you' (*MD* 133/*V* 262), and searches the pockets of Karl's jacket 'with such force that the seams at its side burst' (*MD* 135/*V* 265). '"That's enough," said Karl to himself – his face must have been blushing bright red – and as the head porter, rendered careless by his greed, was poking about in Karl's second pocket, Karl slipped out of his sleeves with a jerk' (*MD* 135/*V* 266).

Throughout the novel, sexuality is a tool of power and oppression. However, the most terrifying exponent of this strategy is not a man but the former opera singer Brunelda. Karl's stay with Brunelda, her lover Delamarche and the feckless Robinson constitutes the novel's darkest part. Exploitation and violence are rife in her apartment, where Karl is a virtual prisoner. When he tries to escape, he is savagely beaten by Delamarche, but more insidious is Brunelda's strategy of psychological manipulation.

When Karl gets out of the car outside her apartment, he immediately finds himself under surveillance: 'Up on the balcony ... a large woman in a red dress got up under the sunshade, took the opera-glass from the ledge, and looked through it at the people below, who only slowly turned their gaze away from her' (*MD* 139/*V* 273). Brunelda occupies a position which in *Meditation* is adopted solely by men: that of the observer at the window who watches the street below with voyeuristic curiosity. The binoculars are a souvenir from Brunelda's career as an opera singer; in fact, she is not just an observer but also a skilled performer. With its makeshift curtains and screens, the small apartment is a stage for Brunelda's one-woman show – her hysterical behaviour, but above all her enormous body, a spectacle in its own right.

Brunelda is one of Kafka's most grotesque characters, a misogynist fantasy made bulging flesh, but she is not the only one of her kind. In fact, Kafka's texts are full of women who shamelessly flaunt their ugly bodies, thereby exerting an irresistible fascination over the men around them. As Kafka writes in his diary, 'I intentionally walk through the streets where there are whores. Walking past them excites me, the remote but nevertheless existent possibility of going with one ... I want only the large, older ones in their outmoded dresses' (19 November 1913; *D* 238/*TB* 594). Disgust in Kafka is a mask for desire; Brunelda, however, is not actually described in great detail. As if to divert attention away from her repulsive but strangely alluring body, the narrative focuses instead on her surroundings: on her clothes and her stuffy, sticky apartment, which is full of rancid food and matted hair – substances either ingested by or expelled from the body. Brunelda's gross corporeality spills over into the world around her. Reading these descriptions, we cannot suppress a shudder, perhaps even a slight gagging reflex, and yet the narrative skilfully keeps these impulses at bay. Just as he represses any sexual urges, Karl fends off any feelings of disgust. 'Your place is so untidy and dirty' (*MD* 185/*V* 363), he admonishes Robinson, but then he calmly starts tidying up and prepares breakfast out of other tenants' half-eaten leftovers.

Even at this low point in his career, then, Karl does not lose heart but applies himself in the hope of finding a better post. It is only in the fragmentary chapter 'Brunelda's Departure' that this drive deserts him. Robinson and Delamarche have disappeared, and it is left to Karl to wheel Brunelda through the city. Their destination is the louche 'Enterprise No. 25', an establishment which to Karl seems fundamentally, irretrievably dirty:

> It was, when you looked more closely, not dirt that you could put your hand on. The stone floor of the hallway had been swept almost clean, the paint on the walls was not old, the artificial palm-trees had only a little dust on them, and yet everything was greasy and repulsive, it was as though everything had been put to a bad use and as if no amount of cleanliness could ever set that right. Karl, whenever he arrived at a new place, liked thinking about what could be improved ... Here, however, he did not know what was to be done. (*MD* 194–5/*V* 384)

The chapter breaks off just a few sentences later. Throughout the novel, Karl is propelled forward by a desire for (self-)improvement, by the desire to clean up his surroundings and his own, sullied past. The disgust which Karl first feels in Johanna Brummer's bed is really self-loathing – his desire to purge himself from those 'dirty' urges which expelled him from the paradise of childhood into the land of adult sexuality. For Karl, this land is America; however hard he tries, Karl sinks deeper and deeper into filth and corruption, until he reaches a place of no return – the brothel, where sexuality can no longer be masked, repressed or ignored.

The Oklahama Theatre: a new beginning?

Kafka abandoned *The Man who Disappeared* in January 1913, but he returned to the manuscript in October 1914 while working on his second novel, *The Trial*. He wrote two short pieces, including 'Brunelda's Departure', but then abandoned the Brunelda storyline and made a fresh start. At a street corner, Karl Rossmann sees a poster advertising a great opportunity. The Theatre of Oklahoma is looking for new staff: 'Everyone is welcome! If you want to be an artist, come along! We are the theatre that can use everyone, each in his place!' (*MD* 195/*V* 387). In its grand promise that anyone is welcome, the theatre advert is reminiscent of the American dream, of the United States as a land of unlimited opportunities, and yet this message is not without ambiguity. The advert ends with the ominous words, 'A curse on anyone who doesn't believe us!' (*MD* 195/*V* 387). As in the case of the sword-bearing Statue of Liberty, welcome and threat go hand in hand.

For Karl, this promise is nonetheless very alluring: 'Everything he had done hitherto was forgotten, nobody would criticize him for it. He could report for a job that was not shameful, but to which, instead, a public invitation was issued!' (*MD* 196/*V* 388). The theatre offers an opportunity for redemption, the forgiveness of previous 'sins' and, sure enough, at the racecourse where the recruitment takes place, Karl is greeted by women dressed as angels who are blowing the trumpet. This chapter has a very different tone and atmosphere from the rest of the novel. Kafka's aim is no longer a realistic depiction of American society; rather, this episode feels slightly unreal, a kind of allegory of Karl's American experience. In the modern, secular age, capitalism is the new religion, or rather its tacky travesty. Utopia, the hope of salvation, is a performance, an advertising ploy, which is alluring but also slightly sinister. For every two hours, the trumpet-blowing women change places with men dressed as devils. America can be heaven, but it can also be hell, with little in between.

In Goethe's *Wilhelm Meister's Apprenticeship* (1795–6), the classic *Bildungsroman*, young Wilhelm joins a travelling theatre troupe on his search for his adult identity. For Wilhelm, the theatre stands for freedom, creativity and self-expression; this hope lives on in Kafka's novel, but only as an impossible ideal. As it turns out, Karl is not allowed to join as an actor, or even as a 'technician', a scaled down version of his original ambition to become an engineer. After a lengthy admissions process, he is eventually sent to the 'office for European secondary-school pupils', 'a booth on the outer edge, not only smaller but also lower than any of the others' (*MD* 202/ *V* 401). Karl is thus admitted on the basis of the qualifications he had when he first arrived in the United States; in the eyes of the theatre he has not progressed but needs to go back to where he first started. However, Karl's admission also speaks of recent humiliation. When asked for his name, he does not give his real name but calls himself 'Negro', 'the name by which he had been called in his last few posts' (*MD* 203/*V* 402). By adopting as his name a term of racist exclusion, Karl aligns himself with one of the most oppressed groups in the America of Kafka's time. Indeed, one of the books Kafka read to familiarize himself with the United States, Arthur Holitscher's travelogue, *America: Today and Tomorrow* (1912), contains a harrowing example of racist persecution: the photograph of the lynching of a black man. The picture bears the poignant caption 'Idyll in Oklahoma'. Holitscher consistently misspelled Oklahoma as 'Oklahama', and the same misspelling occurs in Kafka's novel. Karl's admission into the mysterious Oklahama Theatre, as well as his adopted name 'Negro', provides a tangible link to Holitscher's book, suggesting that the fate awaiting Karl would have been a sinister one.

This sense of foreboding is also tangible in the novel's final, unfinished chapter. Once again Karl is on the move, travelling towards his new workplace by train. His rapid progress makes him realize the size of America, but the landscape outside seems rather hostile: 'Bluish-black masses of stone descended in sharp wedges as far as the train, one leaned out of the window and tried in vain to make out their peaks' (*MD* 211/*V* 418–19). Karl's admission into the Oklahama theatre contains elements of hope, but his train journey into the unknown ends on a distinctly chilly note: 'broad mountain rivers hurried in great waves to the lower slopes . . . and they were so close that the breath of their cold made one's face shiver' (*MD* 211/*V* 419).

Here, Kafka abandons his novel for good, unable to bring his protagonist's journey to a conclusion. Once again, Karl is swept along by events, but this time even he cannot repress a shudder at the fate that awaits him. His inkling may be right. In a diary entry of September 1915, Kafka looks back at his first two novels: 'Rossman and K., the innocent and the guilty, both executed without distinction in the end, the innocent one with a gentler hand, more pushed aside than struck down' (30 September 1915; *D* 343–4/*TB* 757). As in 'The Judgement', *The Metamorphosis* and *The Trial*, death is the only fate that Kafka can envisage for his protagonist. However, it is questionable whether such an ending would have been in keeping with the spirit of the novel. In 1912, Kafka writes to Felice Bauer that his novel is 'designed, I fear, in such a manner that it will never be completed' (11 November 1912; *LF* 49/*BF* 86), suggesting that the travelogue he had in mind was not geared towards a definitive conclusion. This is not to suggest that Kafka was content to leave the novel unfinished; on the contrary, the fact that he returned to the manuscript after a pause of nearly two years suggests his eagerness to tie up its loose ends. And yet it is no coincidence that when Kafka abandons the manuscript for good, Karl is once again on the move. The exhilaration of the creative journey outweighs the satisfaction of arrival.

The Trial

For Kafka, the writing of *The Trial* (*Der Process*, 1914–15) was preceded by a time of personal crisis. After a long-distance relationship lasting one and a half years, he finally got engaged to Felice Bauer in May 1914, but even now he could not shake off his deep-seated doubts about the prospect of marriage. After the official engagement party in Berlin, Kafka writes in his diary, 'Was tied hand and foot like a criminal. Had they sat me down in a corner bound in real chains, placed policemen in front of me and let me look on simply like that, it could not have been worse' (6 June 1914; *D* 275/*TB* 528). These feelings did not go unnoticed. In July, Felice dissolved the engagement in the presence of her sister Erna, the writer Ernst Weiss and her friend Grete Bloch, with whom Kafka had secretly entered into a rather intimate correspondence. Kafka was deeply traumatized by the break-up, which he described as a 'tribunal' (23 July 1914; *D* 293/*TB* 658). The images that Kafka uses in his diary contain the seeds of his second novel. In the middle of August 1914, he embarks on *The Trial*, where the metaphors of arrest and trial become the backbone of the fictional universe.

The actual writing of *The Trial*, however, was preceded by a 'trial run'. On 29 July, Kafka composed a short text featuring a protagonist called Josef K., 'the son of a rich merchant', who is accused by his father of leading a 'dissipated life' (*D* 297/*TB* 666–7). As in 'The Judgement', *The Metamorphosis* and *The Man who Disappeared*, the father in this fragment acts as his son's judge, the family as the site of his trial. In *The Trial*, this role is taken over by the court, although its laws and procedures are just as impenetrable as the motives of Kafka's fathers. In the fragment, we are told what Josef K. is accused of; in the novel, in contrast, Josef K. is never charged with a specific crime and never finds out who accused him. *The Trial*, then, is both bolder and vaguer than this earlier draft, and its unanswered questions become the novel's driving force, the source of its narrative suspense.

The Trial starts with a guess, a speculation: 'Someone must have been telling lies about Josef K., for one morning, without having done anything wrong, he was arrested' (*T* 5/*P* 7). The fact that K. is being arrested without having done 'anything wrong' implies that 'someone' must have been telling lies about him, but the identity of this person is never revealed. This ties in with another ambiguity, which hinges on a grammatical detail. In the original, K.'s innocence is asserted in a phrase which uses the subjunctive ('ohne daß er etwas Böses getan *hätte*'); in German, this form is used in reported speech to indicate that a claim is subjective and potentially unreliable. Kafka's use of the subjunctive *hätte* in the opening sentence has huge implications for the rest of the novel. It suggests that K.'s innocence is not an objective fact but a subjective claim, possibly made by K. himself. In *The Trial*, as in *The Metamorphosis*, Kafka uses a third-person narrator whose perspective is largely identical with that of the protagonist, and yet there are many moments when the narrator subtly relativizes K.'s viewpoint. As readers we can, and must, challenge K.'s take on events.

The novel contains various contradictory statements about the court and the trial. As readers we are never quite sure whom to believe and which information to take literally – and neither is Josef K. He is thrust into the role of the accused, but in the course of the novel he also tries to adopt another part: that of a detective trying to assemble the facts about this case. *The Trial* contains resonances of the metaphysical crime novel, as epitomized by Dostoevsky's *Crime and Punishment* (1866), in which the murderer Raskolnikov comes to confront his own guilt,[7] but Kafka's novel also shares various features with the classic detective story. In a diary entry of 1912, Kafka refers to Sherlock Holmes's dispassionate manner of observation (5 January 1912; *D* 167/*TB* 348–9), and Josef K. tries to adopt a similar stance. He intently watches his surroundings, hoping to derive information about the court from the appearance and behaviour of its officials. But this is a flawed enterprise from the very start. In the first paragraph, we get a detailed description of the guard who has just entered K.'s bedroom: 'He ... was wearing a close-fitting black suit which, like an outfit for travelling, was equipped with a variety of pleats, pockets, buckles, buttons, and a belt that made it appear especially practical, without its precise purpose being clear' (*T* 5/*P* 7). Throughout the novel, K. is trying to decrypt the signs around him, but these signs do not carry a fixed meaning, as they do in a detective story. The guard's outfit is '*like* an outfit for travelling' and '*appear*[s] especially practical', but these might just be K.'s impressions. Ultimately, the real purpose of this garment remains as unclear as the precise mission of its wearer.

The Trial is full of formulations such as 'perhaps', 'probably', 'like' and 'as if', which create a pervading sense of uncertainty. During K.'s interview, the supervisor rearranges the objects on Fräulein Büstner's bedside table 'as if they were objects he needed for the interrogation' (*T* 12/*P* 20). It seems unlikely that these objects are really needed for the interrogation, and yet the supervisor acts *as if* they were. In trying to make sense of his behaviour, K. has to rely on guesswork; the narrative flags up his uncertainty, the provisionality of his interpretations. But the same uncertainty also surrounds K.'s own actions. When he is about to leave Fräulein Bürstner's room at the end of their nocturnal conversation, he hesitates 'as if he hadn't expected to see a door there' (*T* 26/*P* 47). Did K. really not expect to see a door, does he just feign surprise, or does his hesitation have a different meaning altogether? Every so often we are offered an outside perspective on K., but in such moments his actions often appear just as incomprehensible as those of the people around him – to the narrator, the reader and perhaps even to K. himself.

Between dream and reality

The Trial is set in an unnamed modern city. Compared to *The Man who Disappeared*, however, the material aspects of modern life – architecture, transport, technology – are not described in much detail. They provide a backdrop for what is essentially a psychological exploration. *The Trial* is a novel about anonymity, isolation and competition in a society governed by faceless institutions, of which the court is just one example.

Josef K.'s story is strange and unsettling, but he himself is really quite ordinary. K. is an everyman leading an average existence, and this is underlined by his surname, which is shortened to an initial. His life revolves around his work at the bank, where he holds the senior position of first accountant. K. is ambitious and competitive, obsessed with his place in the professional hierarchy; he looks down on his subordinates, tries to impress his boss and is constantly suspicious of his immediate superior and rival, the deputy manager. While the trial comes as a bit of a shock, it does not disrupt his daily routine; in fact, K. decides to treat it like any other business transaction:

> Above all, it was essential, if he was to get anywhere, to discount from the outset any suggestion that he might be guilty. Guilt did not come into it. The trial was nothing more than a piece of business, such as he had often transacted with profit for the bank ... To that end he must not even toy with the thought of guilt, but hold as fast as he could to the thought of his own advantage. (*T* 90/*P* 168)

Treating the trial as 'a piece of business' enables K. to ignore its moral dimension, but while he tries to convince himself that guilt 'did not come into it', the notion keeps creeping back into his thoughts, where it has to be repressed again. By focusing purely on strategic, procedural issues, and above all on his own advantage, K. seeks to control the situation, but with little success. In the course of the novel he attends a hearing, visits the court offices and meets various court officials as well as other people associated with his trial. Each of these episodes starts off with K. in a confident, confrontational mood, but by the end he has lost control and discovers that his assumptions were severely flawed. In some of these cases, K. is let down by a lack of alertness. During his interrogation by the supervisor, he does not not realize that the three men standing in the corner are his colleagues from the bank until this is pointed out to him at the very end. At his first hearing, K. assumes that the audience is divided into two camps and tries to win over both sides, but again it is only right at the end that he spots the differently coloured badges they are all wearing underneath their beards, which suggest that they are all, in fact, part of the same group, with its own complex hierarchy.

Scenes such as these have a surreal, nightmarish quality; the dreamlike character of the novel has often been commented on, but like many such general statements, this needs to be qualified. *The Trial*, like *The Metamorphosis*, starts with the moment of awakening, and this sets the tone for the rest of the novel. Walter Benjamin in his *Arcades Project* (1927–40) speaks of a consciousness 'patterned and checkered by sleep and waking', and adds, 'The first tremors of awakening serve to deepen sleep.'[8] The same pattern can be found in Kafka's texts, where sleep and wakefulness are interlaced in complex, often paradoxical ways, so that the moment of waking leads deep into a world of nightmares.

Indeed, Kafka spells out this danger when he has Josef K. remark to the supervisor that

> it is indeed peculiar that, when one wakes early, one finds, at least in general, everything undisturbed in the same place as the previous night. Indeed, while sleeping and dreaming one has at least apparently been in an essentially different state to being awake, and a boundless presence of mind or rather alertness is needed ... to grasp, upon opening one's eyes, everything in the place where one had relinquished it the previous night. (*PA* 168)

Here Kafka takes another, even more radical step away from the precepts of realism. Not only is his fictional world opaque, resisting the protagonist's attempts to decode it, but it barely exists as an independent, self-contained reality in the first place. Our ordinary lives are neither stable nor 'real', but have to be mentally re-established every day, K. suggests – an undertaking which requires unwavering alertness. According to this reasoning, K.'s trial is not set off by an external event (the 'lies' told by an anonymous informer) but by K. himself, by a momentary slip of attention which derails the normal course of events. Revealingly, Kafka subsequently deleted the passage quoted above – not, arguably, because it is at odds with the rest of the novel, but because it spells out its premise all too clearly.

Although K. regards the court as his enemy, there is, in fact, a strange affinity between him and this institution, which seems to respond to, or even be shaped by, K.'s inner thoughts. In the chapter 'The First Hearing', K. is told that his hearing will take place on Sunday but is given neither the time nor the precise location. At a loose end, K. randomly picks 9 am as a start time, and when he is knocking on various doors in search of the hearing, he pretends to be searching for a carpenter called Lanz. When he finally finds the right room, both of these details are known to the court. Asking once again for the made-up carpenter, K. is immediately admitted by the woman in the antechamber, and the judge in charge reprimands him for being late – K. does not get there until after 10 am. In passages like this, *The Trial* resembles a dream, in which events are shaped by the protagonist's thoughts and feelings. For K., this is not a pleasant experience, nor does it make him feel in control. On the contrary, this mysterious connection between the court and his own mind ties him all the more closely to this institution, which is no longer external to him but seems to extend into the deepest, darkest corners of his self.

In the novel, then, there is no 'outside' to K.'s trial, no place or person that is not in some way connected to it – and hence no way of gaining an objective, outside perspective. In the course of the narrative, he receives lots of advice about his trial, but this advice is fruitless, even contradictory. The painter Titorelli's long speech about the different forms of acquittal suggests that there is a choice to be made; as K. soon realizes, however, these different options postpone the verdict, but none of them leads to a real acquittal. This impasse is underlined by the allegorical painting Titorelli is working on; as K. watches, the Goddess of Justice gradually turns into the Goddess of the Hunt – the court is not impartial and fair but vindictive. Leni makes a similar point. When K. tells her that he is about to go to the cathedral to show around an Italian client, she says suddenly, 'They're hunting you down' (*T* 146/*P* 278). So K. is being chased, hunted down by the court until in the end he is butchered like a dog. But there is another, very different way of describing his relationship with the court. Right at the beginning, the guard tells K. that the court does not actively pursue people but is 'attracted by guilt' (*T* 9/*P* 14). The priest puts it differently again: 'The court does not want anything from you. It receives you when you come and dismisses you when you go' (*T* 160/*P* 304). As readers we are thus faced with different, conflicting ways of describing the relationship between K. and the court. In one version, the court is chasing K.; in another, it is drawn to him because of who he is and how he behaves; and in a third version, it is entirely indifferent to him, receiving him when he enters and releasing him when he leaves. This last model may at first sight seem the most harmless, but in fact it is the most defeatist. Here the court has become synonymous with life itself; the trial of human existence cannot be evaded, and nor can its deadly conclusion.

Playing the part

The multiplicity of different interpretations of court and trial suggests that none of them might be true. This sense of relativism is exacerbated by another theme that runs through the novel, namely theatricality and play-acting. Adopting different roles is part of a child's socialization, but also part of adult life, where we switch between different social roles seamlessly and often without thinking. Role-play – whether in the theatre or in life more generally – can be creative and liberating, but it can also conceal a void, a lack of a stable, 'true' identity.

Neither K. nor the other characters behave entirely naturally. As is indicated by the recurring 'as if' formulations, they all seem to be playing a role, following a secret script. When towards the end of his interrogation K. has regained his confidence, he tells himself that he is in fact 'playing with' the court officials (*T* 14/*P* 26). K. believes that he is in charge of the situation, defining the rules of the game; but is this really the case? Earlier on in the same chapter, it suddenly crosses his mind that his arrest might just be a trick, an elaborate hoax set up by his bank colleagues on the occasion of his thirtieth birthday. K. is unsure whether to play along with this; the text contains a nebulous reference to previous occasions when K., unlike his friends, had behaved 'carelessly and been punished by the outcome', and thus he resolves that 'It was not going to happen again, at least not this time. If it was a hoax, he was going to play along with it' (*T* 7/*P* 12).

Of course, the trial is no hoax, but K.'s resolution sets the tone for the novel, for much of his behaviour can be summed up as trying to 'play along' with a game whose rules he does not understand. To make up for this, K. sometimes tries to create his own rules. When he is alone with Fräulein Bürstner, he starts to re-enact his interrogation: 'I'm the supervisor, two guards are sitting on the trunk over there, and three young men are standing by the photographs ... Oh, I'm forgetting myself, the most important person. Well, I'm standing here, on this side of the table' (*T* 24/*P* 44). Revealingly, K. chooses not to play himself but the Inspector, who 'is sitting very comfortably, legs crossed, one arm draped over the back of the chair'. By re-enacting his interrogation to Fräulein Bürstner, K. tries to regain a sense of control, but before he can get beyond the first line, his own name, he is interrupted by Frau Grubach's nephew, who knocks against the wall.

In other scenes, in contrast, his part is not that of an actor but of a spectator. In the chapter 'Block, the Corn Merchant/The Dismissal of the Lawyer', K. is forced to watch Block grovel at the feet of the lawyer Huld in a sickening display of obedience, but this scene also has a strangely theatrical quality: 'K. had the feeling he was listening to a well-rehearsed dialogue that had been repeated many times before, that would be repeated many times again, and retained its freshness for Block alone' (*T* 139/*P* 264). Repetition is at the heart of performance. Both actors and spectators are trapped in pre-allocated roles, caught up in scenes with a fixed outcome, and everything, including attempted resistance, is just part of this pre-scripted game.

The most surreal example of this repetitive pattern can be found in the chapter 'The Thrasher'. At his first hearing, K. complains about the two guards who arrested him, and a few days later he sees the consequences of his complaint. When he is about to leave the bank in the evening, he discovers the two guards in a lumber-room, where they are forced to strip by the leather-clad thrasher, who bluntly announces: 'I'm employed as a thrasher, so I'll thrash them' (*T* 60/*P* 112). What makes this scene so disturbing is not just its violence, mixed with sexual overtones, but the way it resonates with K.'s thoughts. Deep down, K. probably *wants* the guards to be humiliated, to make up for the way they humiliated him; hence the way in which they are made to strip recalls them supervising K. when he got dressed. But then this unspoken wish becomes horrible, vivid reality. Unable to watch the punishment of the guards, K. shuts the door and runs away – but the next day, he returns. To his horror, when he opens the door, he finds exactly the same scene as the night before.

As Freud argues, the unconscious is a timeless entity, which does not change or evolve. Something similar seems to be going on in the lumber-room. The events in the room are frozen until K. next opens the door; they exist only *for* him. The lumber-room appears to be an extension of K.'s mind, a stage where his secret fantasies of punishment and humiliation are acted out in endless repetition. As K. flees from the lumber-room 'almost in tears', he comes across two messengers, 'who were calmly working at the copying machine' (*T* 62/*P* 117). K. has already encountered the two after his first visit to the lumber-room, but it is only now that the copying machine is mentioned, a detail which alludes to the novel's pattern of narrative replication. But the thrasher episode also contains another self-reflexive reference. When K. first opens the door, he finds 'old, out-of-date printed forms and empty earthenware ink-bottles' strewn across the floor (*T* 58/*P* 108). The lumber-room is a depository for the debris of writing – for scenes which should, perhaps, have been deleted, cleared out, because of their lurid, nightmarish quality, but which are accommodated within the architecture of Kafka's novel, tucked away in one of its most dreamlike corners.

Power and desire

Part of the reason why the thrasher episode is so disturbing lies in its mixture of violence and eroticism. The thrasher's revealing leather outfit, together with the guards' nakedness, lends the scene sado-masochistic overtones; the result is a spectacle designed to captivate the observer, and K.'s decision to return to the room the next day shows that he is indeed captivated. *The Trial* is full of such scenes where K. watches almost against his will; one of the most striking examples occurs in a daydream of K.'s, which is recounted in the unfinished chapter, 'The House'. Wandering through the court building, K. comes across a bullfighter, who struts up and down in one of the antechambers. *The Trial* features a succession of exotic male figures. They include the guard with his tight-fitting travelling suit, the thrasher with his tanned sailor's face and the Italian businessman with his perfumed moustache, all of whom exert a strange fascination over K. In this sequence of ostentatiously paraded male bodies, however, the bullfighter, with his tantalizingly short, tasselled jacket, is the most alluring, and K. is torn between fascination and repulsion:

> K. crept round him, bent low, and gaped at him, straining to keep his eyes wide open. He knew all the patterning of the lace, all the missing tassels ... and could still not take his eyes off it ... he had never wanted to look at it, but it kept a hold on him.   (*T* 184/*P* 350)

The 'it' leaves it open whether K.'s voyeuristic obsession is the result of an inner urge or an external force. In any case, this daydream reveals an insidious mechanism at work within the court. Looking does not ensure detached knowledge but draws the observer ever more deeply into the court's subjugating power.

With one exception, all the court officials in the novel are male, and yet women play an important, unofficial part within the court machinery and its erotically charged atmosphere. The first inkling K. gets that something is amiss is when the women around him no longer behave as they should. Women in

K.'s world serve two purposes: sexual pleasure and domestic comforts. The former is provided by Elsa, a waitress and prostitute whom K. visits once a week, the latter by his landlady Frau Grubach and her cook, although the cook is notable only by her absence. When K. first wakes up, the cook fails to serve him his breakfast; instead, K. notices an old woman at the window opposite, who is watching him 'with quite unusual curiosity' (*T* 5/*P* 7), and who will later follow him from window to window, witnessing his humiliation at the hands of the guards. In Western art, women are often laid out seductively, offered up as an erotic spectacle for the (male) viewer, but here it is the male protagonist who finds himself exposed to the invasive gaze of this old woman.

From the outset, then, K.'s trial unsettles conventional gender roles, even though he tries his best to assert his masculinity. This seems easy at first sight, for he finds himself surrounded by tempting, sexually available women. Thus K.'s initial interrogation takes place not in the living room but in the bedroom of one of his neighbours, Fräulein Bürstner. The Fräulein herself is absent, but her white blouse, at once virginal and seductive, is on display at the window. Under the flimsy pretext of wanting to apologize for the morning's intrusion, K. waits up for her that evening, but once she has asked him into her room, he swiftly moves from apology to seduction, kissing her face and throat until he is interrupted by the knock of Frau Grubach's nephew. Fräulein Bürstner in this scene is tiredly, passively compliant. The women K. meets later on – the wife of the court usher and Leni, Huld's nurse – positively throw themselves on to K., and even the young girls he meets on his way to see the painter Titorelli are sexually precocious, mature well beyond their age.

Of these women, Leni, with her candle and her white apron, is the most mysterious and alluring. K. is particularly fascinated by her webbed fingers, a physical anomaly which points back to an earlier evolutionary stage: 'What a trick of nature', he exclaims, 'What a pretty claw!' (*T* 78/*P* 144). Women in *The Trial* are all body, driven by primal urges, but K. himself is no different. He kisses Fräulein Bürstner's throat 'like a thirsty animal furiously lapping at the water of the spring it has found at last' (*T* 26/*P* 48). Unlike Karl Rossmann, Josef K. is no child but a seasoned seducer, and yet he is often caught off-guard – both by the behaviour of the women around him and by his own response. 'I'm enlisting women helpers', he thinks to himself 'in mild surprise' (*T* 77/*P* 143), but this active verb does not conceal the fact that in his encounters with women his role is almost always the passive one. When Leni pulls him down with her on to the floor, she says triumphantly, 'Now you belong to me' (*T* 78/*P* 146), and K. is put 'in some consternation' by her behaviour: 'Now she was so close to him he could smell the bitter, provocative odour she exuded, like pepper. She took hold of his head, leant across him, and bit and kissed his neck, even bit into his hair' (*T* 78/*P* 146). Here, as in the scene with Fräulein Bürstner, sexual desire manifests itself as consumption, as licking and biting, eating and drinking. The trial stokes K.'s sexual appetites and brings out his animal instincts, but this is neither satisfying nor liberating. On the contrary, throughout the novel, animal imagery is used to highlight a debased form of human existence, full of shame and humiliation.

In his dealings with women, K. is as prone to self-deception as in his dealings with the court, and his confident, even aggressive behaviour quickly gives way to uncertainty. When talking to his landlady, Frau Grubach, he tries to keep up an air of superiority, but is in fact desperate for her 'judgement' and exculpation (*T* 19/*P* 34). Instead of shaking his outstretched hand, however, she merely says: 'Don't take it to heart so, Herr K.' (*T* 19/*P* 35), a remark which deflates K.'s air of indifference. In the course of the novel, K. increasingly relies on the women he meets for help and advice, but this strategy looks increasingly flawed. Whenever he gets involved with a woman there is a male rival lurking in the background, whether this is Frau Grubach's nephew, who disturbs K.'s rendezvous with Fräulein Bürstner, the student who carries away the wife of the court usher, or Huld and Block, who are both involved with Leni. Throughout the novel, K.'s desire is caught up in triangular structures, for the presence of a male rival makes these women seem all the more attractive. K. tries to exploit this situation to his advantage. By seducing women who 'belong' to court officials, he hopes to infiltrate the system, aiming to defeat and humiliate his sexual rivals, but in fact he ends up playing along with the rules of the court.

Right from the start, when he is taken into Fräulein Bürstner's bedroom for his interrogation, K.'s trial is charged with sexual overtones; indeed, it seems that wherever he looks, the world takes on an erotic, obscene tinge. K.'s first hearing is disrupted by the student and the wife of the court usher, who are having sex in the corner, and when K. returns to this room the following weekend, he discovers that the law books on the judge's table are, in fact, crude pornography. 'How dirty everything is here', K. comments. 'And I'm to be judged by people like that?' (*T* 41–2/*P* 76–7). As in *The Man who Disappeared*, 'dirt' is shorthand for seediness and moral corruption, but much of the corruption that K. observes around him is arguably the result of his own, 'dirty' imagination. Talking to Frau Grubach, K. insinuates that Fräulein Bürstner, who often comes home late, might be something of a loose woman, but as soon as his landlady picks up on this point, K. leaves in protest. 'Purity!', he exclaims on his way out, 'If you want to keep the guest-house pure, you'll have to give me notice first of all' (*T* 21/*P* 37). Guilt and moral corruption can no longer be safely attributed to others. Rather, *The Trial* operates according to a logic of contagion; whenever K. points the finger at others, he himself emerges sullied and tainted, just as the lust and obscenity which surround him mirror his own inner life.

'Before the Law'

The Trial does not have a clear narrative arch or trajectory; in fact, to this day the intended order of its chapters remains unclear. K.'s encounters with different people do not achieve any material progress; rather, each scene merely adds to the growing sense of confusion and defeatism. In the penultimate chapter, 'In the Cathedral', the mood is particularly ominous, filled with a sense of foreboding. The atmospheric setting of the dark, empty cathedral contributes to this, as do various details, most notably an altarpiece of Christ's burial, whose subject K. gradually pieces together with the help of his torch. This painting anticipates what is to come, but K. does not dwell on its meaning. He is more captivated by the story that he is told by the priest – the story about the 'man from the country' who has come to gain entrance to the Law. The doorkeeper guarding its entrance, however, tells him that he cannot 'now' be admitted. The man is a sketchy figure without a name or a past; the doorkeeper is described in a little more detail, but ultimately his role, character and intentions remain equally hazy. Neither side is willing to budge, and after years of waiting by the entrance, the man dies, only to be told by the doorkeeper in his dying moments: 'this entrance was intended for you alone. I shall now go and shut it' (*T* 155/*P* 294–5).

The story thus ends with a paradox. The door is open, an entrance designated for this man alone, and yet during his lifetime he is not allowed to pass through it. But this is just one of several puzzles. The man has the epithet 'from the country'; does this imply that the Law is located in the city? We get no indication of the wider context. More important still, perhaps, what *is* 'the Law', and what is the man hoping to achieve once he has gained access to it? The existence of door and doorkeeper suggests that the Law is some kind of building, but to imagine it as a court building, or perhaps an archive or library, would surely be reductive.

In his dying moment, the man sees a light emanating from inside the Law, although it remains unclear whether his failing eyes are deceiving him. As readers we are in a similar situation. The priest's story appears at a decisive point in the novel, in the chapter before K.'s execution, and seems to have an obvious relevance for K.'s own case, and yet we are unsure how exactly to relate it to his trial. There are various parallels between K. and the man from the country – such as their reliance on questionable authority figures and their eventual death – but there are also disparities. The Law is not identical to the court, and whereas the court intrudes on K.'s life, arresting and eventually executing him, the man comes to the Law apparently out of his own free will.

The story's purpose within the novel is thus itself a puzzle, perhaps even a decoy. According to the priest, the story is part of the 'introduction to the Law', a kind of preamble. It too is situated '*before* the Law', a passageway into the corpus of the law, but one which – like the literal door in the story – turns out to be a barrier, a stumbling block. Kafka referred to the story as a legend, and in Kafka criticism it is sometimes called a parable, a text containing a particular lesson. Walter Benjamin problematizes this term. The narrative of *The Trial*, he argues, can be read as 'the unfolding of the parable', not in the sense of a piece of paper being flattened out, but rather of a bud opening into a blossom.[9] The discussion between K. and the priest illustrates the tension between these two models of unfolding. K. wants to 'flatten out' the parable, reduce it to a single point. 'So the doorkeeper deceived the man', he responds immediately, and insists, 'but it's obvious', even when the priest warns that he should not be too rash (*T* 155/*P* 295). In fact, the priest does not confirm any of K.'s interpretations, but reveals layer upon layer of additional meaning. In doing so, he does not once offer his own interpretation, but merely reports the views of an unspecified group of 'explicators' (*T* 155/*P* 296). He starts his explanations with phrases such as 'opinions vary as to whether' and 'but many agree that' (*T* 158/*P* 301). The conversation between K. and the priest is thus accompanied by a choir of anonymous voices, some of them unified, others in discord. As the priest shows – to K.'s frustration – interpretation is a messy, open-ended process rather than a linear journey towards the truth. In this it resembles K.'s trial, where a final verdict is never spoken but where, as the priest tells K., 'the proceedings gradually turn into the verdict' (*T* 152/*P* 289).

While the story itself has various affinities with Jewish legends, its subsequent interpretation resonates with the Jewish scholarly tradition. The Talmud is a commentary on Jewish scripture primarily concerned with Judaic law. In it, an extract from the Torah is typically surrounded by rabbis' comments, which in turn are annotated by further comments, all of which are studied and annotated by Talmudic scholars. The primary text and its interpretations, then, form part of the same textual corpus, and the process of interpretation and commentary continues indefinitely. K. is disheartened by this lack of closure, for he wants certainty, a definitive interpretation. Within the framework of Kafka's novel, however, this model of the multivalent text and its open-ended interpretation has, as we will see, a particular, crucial purpose.

'The End'

When he gave up on his novel, probably in late January 1915, Kafka had produced about 280 handwritten pages, 200 of which date from the first two months, when work was progressing quickly. *The Trial* remains incomplete, but it is not strictly speaking un*finished*. Unlike *The Man who Disappeared* and *The Castle*, it actually has a conclusion, for Kafka took the unusual step of writing the first and last chapters first, followed by the intervening episodes. The novel's German title, *Der Process*, means both 'the trial' and 'the process'; by writing the conclusion up front, Kafka tries to contain the writing process, preventing it from becoming interminable and open-ended.

Revealingly, both the novel and the priest's story end with the death of the protagonist. Closure is achievable, but at what cost? The final chapter, which is called simply 'The End', contains a covert reference to this problem. As K. is walked to his execution by the two men who have come to fetch him, they hook their arms into his: 'K. walked between them, stiffly upright, the three of them forming such a single unit that destroying one of them would have meant destroying them all. It was a kind of unit only inanimate objects can usually form' (*T* 161/*P* 306). Here the concept of narrative unity is transplanted into the text. K. is framed by his executioners, but this unit of bodies takes on an inhuman quality. Only lifeless things, the text implies, can achieve such perfect unity. Framed in such a way, the body (of the text) turns into a corpse, and the only reaction against this rigor mortis is violence, destruction. This passage sums up the dilemma at the heart of Kafka's creative vocation. The finished, publishable work is something that Kafka strives for, and yet this self-contained form is incompatible with the organic model of writing that Kafka describes in relation to 'The Judgement' – writing as an ecstatic, sensual experience, a continuous stream that can be neither controlled nor contained.

Kafka's method of writing the first and last chapters first is reflected in the narrative. 'The Arrest' and 'The End' have close thematic links, and together they provide a tightly structured frame for the rest of the novel. The final chapter is set on the eve of K.'s thirty-first birthday, exactly one year after his arrest, and is informed by an uncanny sense of repetition. In both chapters, for instance, windows play a central role. One of the first things Josef K. notices when waking up at the beginning is the nosy old woman in the flat opposite, who, together with her two male companions, follows K. from window to window, anxious not to miss a moment of his arrest. The last chapter, in contrast, is set in the evening, at 'the time when the streets are quiet' (*T* 161/*P* 305), and now the only people visible in the house opposite are two toddlers, who are playing in a lit window. As K's own life is drawing to a close, the age of the people in the building opposite decreases from old to very young. In the opening chapter, K. is annoyed by his neighbours' curiosity, but the sight of the young children is even more unsettling. They are tied to the spot, unable to move or touch each other, and the window in which they are sitting has got bars – a reflection of K.'s own entrapment and isolation.

This window scene is inserted into a passage which describes K.'s first encounter with his executioners. K. was arrested by two guards, and at the end he is again visited by two court representatives: men in top hats and black suits who are reminiscent of undertakers. At the beginning of the novel, the guards surprise K., who is still in bed, dressed in his nightshirt, but this time he is fully prepared. He is dressed for the occasion in a black suit, which matches the men's funeral outfits, and pulls on new tight-fitting gloves. K. has come a long way since his arrest. Although he still has not understood the reason behind his trial, it seems that, at the end, he has come to accept its rules and expectations.

Even this final chapter, however, with its mood of resignation, is shot through with moments of defiance. When K. first meets the two men, he admits to himself 'that he had expected different visitors' (*T* 161/*P* 306). We are not told whom or what K. had been expecting, but he seems to have a preconception of what the men coming to fetch him should look like. The reality, as so often with the court, is disappointing, even off-putting. Looking at them closely, K. 'found the cleanliness of their faces nauseating. One could positively see the cleansing fingers that had poked in the corners of their eyes, rubbed their upper lips, and scraped out the folds under their chins' (*T* 162/*P* 307). This passage harks back to the sight of the two toddlers; K.'s executioners are like young children whose faces need to be washed by others. Throughout his trial, K. is repulsed by the (literal and metaphorical) dirt which he comes to associate with the court; the men's cleanliness, however, is even more repulsive, for the imagined cleaning process evokes – foreshadows – another scene: the washing of a corpse.

K.'s executioners, then, are strangely lifeless, moving and acting as one, like robots, but in K. this also evokes another association. 'They send old, second-rate actors for me', he thinks, in disappointment; 'they're trying to get rid of me on the cheap' (*T* 161/*P* 306). Images of play-acting recur throughout the novel, but at this late, poignant moment the effect is particularly disconcerting. If the court enlists only second-rate actors for its final task, this turns the deadly serious event of K.'s execution into a cheap spectacle. K. tries to protest, but in vain. 'At which theatre are you engaged?' he asks the two (*T* 161/*P* 306), but his question remains unanswered, and they carry on with their task. Even to spell out the theatricality of events, to try to step out of the 'theatrical illusion' of the trial, cannot stop the horrific scene which is about to unfold. Everything, including K.'s resistance, is part of the game.

As a result, K. quickly stops trying to resist. Although he was initially trying to stall, he soon starts leading the way to his execution, pulling the other two along so fast that they can hardly keep up. K.'s behaviour here is strange, but it is not unprecedented. In the thrasher episode, he cannot help returning to the lumber-room the next day, and after initially resisting the priest's call, he suddenly turns around and runs towards him across the empty cathedral. In the last chapter, he finally lets his attraction to the court have free rein. Not only are he and the two men now walking 'fully in accord', it is K. who is leading the way through the city and out of it.

Eventually they stop at a deserted quarry, a site reminiscent of the inhospitable mountain range through which Karl Rossmann travels at the end of *The Man who Disappeared*. Both are 'natural' spaces, but lacking in vegetation or any other sign of life. The setting of Josef K.'s execution is inspired by an article which Kafka wrote for the Workers' Accident Insurance Institute in 1914 to highlight the unsafe working conditions in quarries. The report contains fifteen photographs; in his text, Kafka comments on them in unusually expressive language which departs from the sober style associated with an insurance report:

> The sight of this quarry is alarming. Debris, rubble and refuse cover everything in sight ... The debris above where [the worker] is standing ... collapsed during the thaw of March 1914. Fortunately, the workers were having their afternoon coffee at the time of the collapse, or all of them would have been buried alive.   (*O* 291/*A* 405)

Kafka wrote this report in 1914, the year when he was working on *The Trial*, and the quarry as a site of lethal danger recurs at the end of his novel. However, while the tone of Kafka's insurance report is dramatic, the novel's conclusion is strikingly, chillingly, understated. Here, the quarry is the site not of looming accidents but of a carefully prepared execution. In fact, the mood is tranquil, almost idyllic: 'Everything was bathed in moonlight, with the naturalness and calm no other light possesses' (*T* 163/*P* 310). And while the quarries in Kafka's report are full of rubble, here the only detail reminiscent of this chaos is the one 'stone ... that had broken off', on which K. will be killed (*T* 164/*P* 311).

Up to now, K. has been compliant, but now his composure is beginning to crack. He shudders as the two men undress him, and as he rests his head on the stone, his posture remains, 'despite all the cooperation K. showed ... very strained and unconvincing' (*T* 164/*P* 311). Rather than words, it is K.'s body which speaks out against the trial's inhumanity. And yet the ending is ambivalent, containing both tragic elements and details which defy the conventions of tragedy. K.'s executioners may be second-rate actors, but K.'s own dying performance is equally lacking in tragic gravitas. As the two men pass the butcher's knife between themselves, 'K. knew very well that it would have been his duty to grasp the knife himself . . . and plunge it into his own body' (*T* 164/ *P* 308). K. knows the conventions of classical tragedy, the role of the noble hero embracing his own death, but in the end, his own dying role is very different. 'Like a dog!' he says as the knife is twisted in his heart, and the narrator adds, 'it seemed as if his shame would live on after him' (*T* 165/*P* 312). After the drawn-out and strangely inconclusive episodes that make up the rest of the novel, K.'s execution is sudden and shocking in its brutality, which would have been as disturbing to Kafka's contemporaries as it is to modern readers. And yet on another level, K.'s death does not come completely out of the blue; rather, it is a more brutal replay of merchant Block's performance as 'the lawyer's dog' (*T* 139/*P* 265). As he was watching Block humiliate himself, K. could not help thinking that 'the observer almost felt degraded' by this spectacle (*T* 139/*P* 264). Little did he know that soon it would be his own shame which would outlive his dying performance. With *The Trial*, Kafka succeeded in writing a novel with a conclusion, and yet K.'s death points beyond the end, infecting the reader with its lingering sense of shame. *The Trial* is a theatre of cruelty, a succession of lurid scenes of sex, punishment and humiliation in which everyone is complicit, whether actor or spectator.

'In the Penal Colony' and *A Country Doctor*

'In the Penal Colony'

While working on *The Trial*, Kafka also wrote the short story 'In the Penal Colony' ('In der Strafkolonie', 1914), a kind of exotic counterpart to his novel. Once again, we are confronted with a penal system that is opaque and unjust, but this story is even more disturbing than *The Trial*. Physical violence, which in the novel plays a relatively small part, here takes centre stage in a drawn-out description of torture and execution. Unlike *The Trial*, however, the text is not set in a Western city but in the eponymous penal colony, an unnamed, remote desert island. This island is visited by a traveller who gets drawn into a conflict between tradition and progress. A new commandant has taken over who wants to abolish the old, barbaric system of execution introduced by his predecessor, whereby the convicted person is slowly tortured to death by a machine that tattoos the sentence on to the man's naked body. The traveller is treated to a live demonstration by the officer, the former commandant's last faithful representative. At first, the execution seems imminent, but when the traveller refuses to defend this penal system to the new commandant, the officer aborts the execution and puts himself under the machine, which self-destructs in the process of killing him.

'In the Penal Colony' scandalized Kafka's contemporaries with its graphic violence and the pedantic, detached manner in which the torture mechanism is described – a tone familiar from the insurance reports on industrial working conditions which Kafka would have read and written for the Insurance Institute. In a 1920 review, the writer Kurt Tucholsky commented that the story leaves a 'stale taste of blood' in the mouth of its reader, who seeks refuge from its violence through non-literal, allegorical interpretations.[10] The tale has indeed attracted a wide range of critical approaches, ranging from cultural-historical readings via post-colonial approaches to deconstruction.

Historical studies have traced the possible sources which could have inspired Kafka's unusual text. They include literary models such as Octave Mirbeau's scandalous pornographic novel, *The Torture Garden* (1899), as well as reports about contemporary penal colonies such as Devil's Island off the Coast of French Guinea. The use of penal colonies was also hotly debated in Germany and Austria at the time. Kafka's former law professor, Hans Gross, propagated the deportation of 'degenerate' elements of society, and in 1909 the German government commissioned a report on penal colonies, which was conducted by the young lawyer Robert Heindl. In his book, *My Journey to the Penal Colonies* (1913), Heindl stressed that his account was intended to offer a dispassionate look at different penal systems without being 'distracted' by sympathy with the deported.

The traveller in Kafka's story could be modelled on Heindl. Initially he is detached, even bored, and even as he becomes increasingly repulsed by the machine's cruelty and injustice, he remains unsure whether to interfere, 'for he was travelling simply as an observer and not with the smallest intention of changing the legal constitution of a foreign country' (M 85/DL 222). Listening to the officer's elaborate plan to restore the machine to its old glory, he decides to speak up against the system towards the new commandant. At the scene, however, he remains trapped in the position of observer, and even when the officer puts himself under the machine, he does nothing to stop him. For us readers, the traveller is an ambivalent figure of identification. We share his growing sense of repulsion, and yet his impassive behaviour uncomfortably suggests cowardice dressed up as impartiality. Like the traveller, we watch the unfolding spectacle with morbid fascination. Even more than in *The Trial*, Kafka's story elides the difference between protagonist and reader, forcing us to share in the observer's voyeuristic guilt.

Given the exotic setting, the story also has a more specifically colonial subtext. Ostensibly, the narrative is structured around the opposition between the enlightened Western traveller and the strange rituals of an 'exotic' society. In fact, however, the (penal) colonies were of course a European creation, and the torture machine is an emblem of modern technology, of human progress at its most advanced and destructive. When he describes the 'Bed' on to which the prisoner is strapped to be tortured by the 'Harrow', the officer remarks, 'you will have seen similar apparatuses in private clinics' (*M* 78/*DL* 209) – a comment as casual as it is disturbing. Here Kafka's text anticipates the work of the French philosopher Michael Foucault, who emphasized the similarities between different kinds of modern institutions such as prisons, schools, hospitals and asylums, all of which are designed to discipline, control and condition the individual.

Kafka wrote the story in the autumn of 1914, two months after the beginning of the First World War, which was dominated by technological warfare. Critics have looked for specific inventions which could have inspired Kafka's depiction of the machine, but one focal point of interpretations is the fact that the torture machine is, in fact, a writing machine, which tattoos the prisoner's sentence on to his naked body, killing him in the process. A similar link between writing and death is made in the short story 'A Dream' ('Ein Traum'), written between 1914 and 1916, in which the protagonist, Josef K., sees his name appear in gold letters on a tombstone just as he lets himself fall into the pre-dug grave (*DL* 298). Writing in both texts is incompatible with life, a destructive but also redemptive force with the power to transform the mortal body into something more perfect and permanent. Josef K.'s name appears in ornate gold letters, and the sentence tattooed on to the prisoner's body is a calligraphic work of art, which cannot even be deciphered by the naked eye. This detail, however, underlines the deep ambiguity of this image. The text, the artwork, that takes the place of the living body may be beautiful and enthralling, but if underneath its beauty it is indecipherable and ultimately senseless, is it really worth the sacrifice? The officer enthusiastically describes the moment of 'transfiguration' experienced by the prisoner when he deciphers the sentence with his wounds (*M* 87/*DL* 226), but his own face in death speaks a very different language:

> It was as it had been in life; not a sign of the promised deliverance was to be discovered; what all the others had found in the machine, the officer had not found; his lips were pressed tight; his eyes were open, and had the appearance of life; his gaze was calm with conviction; the point of a great iron spike pierced his brow.   (*M* 98/*DL* 245–6)

A Country Doctor

'In the Penal Colony' marks a transitional point in Kafka's work. Kafka envisaged publishing it, together with 'The Judgement' and *The Metamorphosis*, in a volume entitled 'Punishments' ('Strafen'), suggesting a thematic link with his earlier writings. Yet 'In the Penal Colony' also departs from the previous texts in ways which anticipate the themes of his middle period, of the short stories written in 1916–17 and beyond. These stories are much more diverse in terms of subject-matter, tone and style; many take us away from the modern European setting of the earlier texts into unfamiliar terrain, and some do not even feature a human protagonist.

After over a year of writing very little, Kafka experienced another burst of creativity in 1916–17. His sister Ottla had rented a small cottage near the Prague castle, which she offered Kafka as a writing retreat. This change of location proved very fruitful; between November 1916 and May 1917 Kafka composed about twenty short prose texts, as well as the drama fragment 'The Warden of the Tomb' ('Der Gruftwächter'). Kafka pursued the publication of these texts with unusual determination. In February 1917 he started to compile lists of texts which could make up a volume of short stories, and in July he sent thirteen pieces to his publisher, Kurt Wolff. Wolff took on the project, but publication of the volume was dogged by various delays, and *A Country Doctor* (*Ein Landarzt*) did not appear until May 1920.

Kafka took great care over the selection of the stories and changed the order a few times. So how coherent a volume is *A Country Doctor*? Its texts, and other pieces written around the same time, are thematically diverse but linked by recurring ideas, some of which I shall discuss here.

Outsiders: animals and artists

Kafka's animals are strange yet strangely familiar. The creatures featured in his texts – horses, mice and dogs and, at the more exotic end of the spectrum, apes, panthers and jackals – are not in themselves particularly unusual. What makes them unsettling is the manner of their textual representation. As Walter Benjamin remarks:

> You can read Kafka's animal stories for quite a while without realizing that they are not about human beings at all. When you finally come upon the name of the creature – monkey, dog, mole – you look up in fright and realize that you are already far away from the continent of man.[11]

The shock described by Benjamin springs from a blurring of categories, the fact that Kafka's animal stories are not always instantly recognizable as such. Some feature human narrators who are confronted with strange and unsettling creatures, but in other texts animals are themselves narrators, drawing us into their way of thinking. From their perspective, it is the world of humans which is strange and off-putting. Kafka's animal stories challenge our established views of humans *and* animals in ways which are both unsettling and illuminating. By removing us from the 'continent of man', Kafka's texts give us the chance to discover this continent anew.

The volume's opening story, 'The New Advocate' ('Der neue Advokat'), closely fits Benjamin's description, for here the animal nature of the protagonist is mentioned almost in passing. As the unnamed narrator explains, 'We have a new advocate, Doctor Bucephalus. There is little in his outward appearance to recall the time when he was Alexander of Macedon's battle-charger' (*HA* 12/*DL* 251). Bucephalus was the battle horse of Alexander the Great (356–323 BC), King of Macedon, who created one of the largest empires in the ancient world. Kafka's story doubly displaces this historic animal: from antiquity into modern times and from Alexander's battlefields to the world of law courts and libraries. Yet the precise extent of Bucephalus' transformation remains unclear. We are told that 'little in his outward appearance' recalls his time as a battle-charger, though the narrator adds cryptically, 'True, there are a few things that someone acquainted with the circumstances will notice' (*HA* 12/*DL* 251). This sentence is a kind of reading instruction. The text gives us no description of Bucephalus' appearance, and we thus have to extrapolate information from small details, such as the fact that he climbs the stairs 'step by ringing marble step', a formulation which evokes horseshoes rather than human feet.

In the second paragraph, the narrator compares Alexander's times with the present day. Although intrigues and conflicts have survived, the present lacks a charismatic leader who could point the way to a new destination. The clear-cut hierarchies of ancient times, the text implies, have given way to the labyrinth of modern bureaucracy, although this change is not all bad. The text's closing image is of Bucephalus studying law books, 'free, flanks unconfined by the rider's thighs, in the quiet of the lamplight, far from the tumult of Alexander's battle' (*HA* 12/*DL* 252). By adopting a human profession, Bucephalus has shed the rider who previously controlled his every move. Indeed, his new-found freedom is arguably greater than that of most humans. As a legal scholar, he has escaped the battlefields of the past as well as the pressures of modern life through a mixture of adaptation and withdrawal.

In 'Jackals and Arabs' ('Schakale und Araber'), the encounter between man and animal takes place in the wilderness of the Arabian desert. This remote setting is seen through the eyes of a European traveller, who gets drawn into the age-old conflict between Arabs and jackals.

The text begins in a dreamlike mode. After his companions have gone to sleep, the narrator finds himself surrounded by a horde of jackals, one of whom tells him their story. Through the ages, the jackals have waited for his arrival, for only a person from 'the north' has the power to free them from their plight – from a life of exile among the Arabs, whose physical presence and barbaric customs disgust the jackals and destroy their peace. To end their plight, they present the traveller with a pair of small, rusty sewing scissors with which he should cut the Arabs' throats, but then they are interrupted by a whip-wielding Arab. He confirms the animals' story about the conflict between jackals and Arabs but debunks the jackals' self-image as pure and rational creatures. When the Arab has the corpse of a camel thrown nearby, the jackals are all drawn to it 'irresistibly as if by a rope' (*HA* 24/*DL* 275), devouring it with animalistic greed.

The story first appeared in Martin Buber's periodical *The Jew* (*Der Jude*), a forum for Jewish culture and debate, and has often been read as a (deeply ambiguous) parable about modern Jewish identity. 'Jackals and Arabs' chimes with the contemporary Zionist argument that without a designated homeland the Jewish people are forced to live in permanent exile, dependent on the tolerance of their 'host nation'. In fact, this notion was also part of anti-Semitic propaganda, which compared Jewish people to jackals – parasites feasting on other creatures' blood. This image features prominently in Hitler's *Mein Kampf*, but it also appeared in nineteenth-century literary texts by both Jewish and non-Jewish authors, where such images are used playfully and subversively.

Kafka refines the jackal analogy through several details. His jackals, like the Jewish people, are matrilineal, and their revulsion at the Arabs' slaughtering practice alludes to Jewish purity laws. Most important, a core element of Judaism (as of Christianity) is its belief in a messiah, a saviour who will come and redeem his chosen people. Kafka's story, however, debunks the jackals' hope for a saviour from 'the north' as hopeless and naïve. The small rusty scissors are a ludicrous weapon, and the traveller is a reluctant messiah who refuses to be drawn into this conflict. Most important, by propagating this 'messianic' solution, the jackals undermine their own self-image as rational, pure and non-violent creatures.

'Jackals and Arabs' is reminiscent of 'In the Penal Colony', for in both texts a Western traveller gets caught up in a conflict between two opposing groups. Both travellers try to stay neutral and open-minded, but neither can quite conceal his own violent tendencies. At the end of 'In the Penal Colony', the traveller stops the soldier and the freed prisoner from following him on to his ship by threatening them with a rope, which he holds like a whip (*DL* 248). In 'Jackals and Arabs' an actual whip is wielded by the Arab to dispel the jackals, and the traveller shares his attitude. When he first sees the jackals approaching, they appear to him as a group of 'slender bodies, their movements drilled and nimble as if driven by a whip' (*HA* 22/*DL* 270). Even when we encounter animals in the wild, this image implies, we impose on them our deeply ingrained desire for domestication.

Like the opening text 'The New Advocate', the long closing piece of the *Country Doctor* collection, 'A Report to an Academy' ('Ein Bericht für eine Akademie'), is a story about transformation. In order to escape life in a cage, the captured ape Rotpeter decides to become human, or rather, to adopt human behaviour. His story is a narrative experiment: how does socialization happen outside the family, as a conscious choice rather than a gradual, unconscious process? Kafka was very interested in pedagogy, in the processes through which a child is integrated into society, and describes himself in one childhood photograph as 'my parents' ape' (28 November 1912; *LF* 94/*BF* 138). While in this image the child imitating his parents is a metaphorical ape, in 'A Report to an Academy' an actual ape takes on human characteristics by 'aping' the people around him. But Kafka's letter also anticipates the story in another respect. The verb *auftreten*, which Kafka uses to describe his childhood self, means 'to appear as' but also 'to perform'. The child mimicking his parents is not just an ape but an actor. This ambiguity is carried through into the story of the ape, whose imitation of human behaviour is both demeaning and subversive.

Rotpeter's first role models are the sailors on the ship, from whom he learns the art of smoking, drinking and spitting. Viewed through the eyes of the animal, human nature seems neither noble nor civilized but crude and debased. In this respect, Rotpeter follows in a well-established tradition; in art and literature, apes are often used as a satirical mirror of human behaviour. After his transformation, Rotpeter becomes the star of a variety show, but apart from smoking and drinking, he is also capable of more refined behaviour. His account is a lecture, perhaps his most accomplished and subversive performance, which he delivers to the learned members of an academy. 'A Report to an Academy' is one of Kafka's most theatrical texts and has been adapted for the stage as a dramatic monologue.

Language, then, is vital for Rotpeter's transformation. A tool of communication and self-expression, it enables him to enter the human world and tell his own story, but it also imposes inescapable restrictions. Language is based on a set of conventions; in order to make ourselves understood we have to use words that are used by everyone around us. In Rotpeter's case, moreover, language also points to a trauma which is encapsulated in his name, 'Red Peter'. While he chose to become human, he did not choose his own name, which was given to him by his captors and is inspired by the red scar left on his face by a shotgun wound. The ape's name, then, is itself a kind of scar, a reminder of the violence which catapulted him out of his animal existence into the world of language.

At first sight, Rotpeter's is a success story, a Darwinist story of survival through adaptation, but when we look more closely, we find evidence of loss and failure: the loss of his animal identity, and his failure to become fully part of human society. The ape has managed to escape his cage, but has not actually become human; rather, he is stuck somewhere in-between, a hybrid or freak who belongs to neither world. At night, when he comes home from his show, he is reminded of his true self by his companion, a half-tame chimp who has 'the crazy, confused look of the trained animal in her eyes' (*HA* 45/*DL* 314). In order to survive, the ape has had to leave behind 'my origins . . . my memories of my youth' (*HA* 38/*DL* 299), and the door leading back to his animal past has grown so small, 'I would have to skin the fur off my back to get through it' (*HA* 38/*DL* 300). To return to his original state, Rotpeter would have to shed his fur – a paradox which shows that the past is forever out of reach.

That said, the way forward is equally restricted. The horse-lawyer Bucephalus is presented as 'free', but the ape's aims are much more modest. All he wants is 'a way out':

> I use the word in its fullest and most customary sense. I deliberately do not say freedom. I do not mean this great feeling of freedom on all sides. Perhaps as an ape I may have known it, and I have been acquainted with humans who yearn for it. But for my own part I had no desire for freedom, neither then nor today. (*HA* 40/*DL* 304)

Rotpeter is one of Kafka's most pragmatic protagonists. Characters such as Josef K. in *The Trial* are obsessed with (re-)gaining their freedom but fail to recognize that this freedom never existed in the first place. Their stories often have a lethal outcome; Rotpeter, on the other hand, survives because he has accepted the constraints of his existence. As he concludes, 'I feel more comfortable and included [*eingeschlossener*, which also means "locked in"] in the human world' (*HA* 38/*DL* 299).

Like 'Jackals and Arabs', 'A Report to an Academy' was first published in Martin Buber's journal *The Jew*. Kafka's friend Max Brod was the first of many critics who have read the text as a satire of Jewish assimilation. Young Jews of Kafka's generation were increasingly critical of the ways their parents had become assimilated into mainstream Western society, thereby betraying their religious and cultural roots. 'A Report to an Academy' chimes with these debates and reflects Kafka's own growing engagement with his Jewish identity. Yet while Rotpeter's case illustrates the costs of assimilation, its implications reach far beyond the Jewish context, and Kafka himself resisted an allegorical reading of the story. In a letter, he politely rejects Buber's suggestion of printing the two stories under the heading 'Two Parables', suggesting instead the more neutral 'Two Animal Stories' (12 May 1917; *LFFE* 132/*B3* 299).

For Rotpeter, performance underpins not just his variety act but his entire existence. The much shorter text 'In the Gallery' ('Auf der Galerie') is also set in the circus milieu, but it focuses on one act: the performance of an equestrienne and her male ringmaster. In fact, the story offers two versions of this scene. The first description casts this scene in a bleak light, as a case of drudgery and exploitation, while the second matches the more conventional notion of the circus as a bright and cheerful place. Ultimately, though, both versions are exaggerated, and while the second is presented as the truth, the ending challenges any clear-cut distinction between reality and illusion.

The text consists of only two paragraphs, each of which is made of one long sentence. In the first, the performer, 'some frail, consumptive circus rider', is driven round the ring on her swaying horse by the sadistic ringmaster. With his whip, he resembles a slave driver, supported in his efforts by 'an unflagging audience' and accompanied by 'the incessant roaring of orchestra and ventilators' (*HA* 18/*DL* 262). Kafka's use of participle constructions – the equestrienne is 'pirouetting on her horse, throwing kisses, swaying from the waist' – conveys a sense of endless, circular motion. This scenario threatens to continue 'into the ever-widening grey future', but then the syntactical flow is suddenly disrupted. Introduced by a dash, a new character enters the scene: 'perhaps then a young spectator would rush down the long set of steps through all the rows, dash into the ring and cry "Stop!" through the fanfares of the ever accommodating orchestra' (*HA* 18/*DL* 262).

Here the first paragraph ends. The young spectator might put an end to this nightmarish scene, but this is by no means certain, for his interference hinges on a precarious 'perhaps'. This tentative conclusion is in tune with the rest of the sentence. Starting with 'If', this is not a factual description but a thought-experiment in which the equestrienne's hypothetical plight *might* in turn lead to her rescue by the young visitor. The indicative is used only once, in the description of the 'falling and fresh-rising clapping of applauding hands that *are* really steam-hammers' (my emphasis). This odd, defamiliarizing comparison is the one certainty in an otherwise hypothetical scenario. Grammatically speaking, then, the first paragraph is highly unusual, and yet the story it tells is fairly conventional. A damsel in distress is rescued by a male hero, a fairytale prince who breaks the (ring)master's evil spell.

This narrative is dismissed in the second paragraph with the blunt assertion 'But as that is not the way it is.' The scene is then revisited from an entirely different perspective. This time the circus rider is not a frail girl but 'a lovely lady, white and red', and the ringmaster is an admiring figure. After a triumphant performance, she basks in the audience's applause, sharing her happiness with the entire circus. So far, this second paragraph offers a reassuring revision of the first, bleak scene, replacing a bad dream with a more cheerful reality. But then the syntax is again disrupted by a dash, which introduces a change of scene, shifting the focus to the gallery: 'as this is the way it is, the young spectator lays his head on the railing, and sinking into the final march as into a deep dream, he weeps, without being aware of it' (*HA* 18/ *DL* 263).

How are we to read this ending? If the reality is cheerful rather than sinister, why does the young spectator put his head down and cry? His tears suggest a crisis of masculinity. The modern woman does not need to be rescued by a knight in shining armour. But this feminist reading is subtly undermined in the text, for although the rider is introduced as 'a lovely lady', she is later down-graded to 'the little one' (*HA* 18/*DL* 263), fussed over by the ringmaster 'as if she were his best-loved granddaughter' (*HA* 18/*DL* 262). The rider remains caught up in a traditional framework in which the ringmaster maintains a patriarchal authority.

The visitor's incongruous response provides a kind of meta-comment on the narrative. On the face of it, the story moves from dream to reality, but then the visitor's dreamy tears at the end implicitly refer us back to the beginning. Just as horse and rider go round in circles, so the ending sets in motion a circular reading process. As the title indicates, the main focus of Kafka's text is not on the events in the arena but on the spectator. Ultimately the story presents not two alternative versions but two complementary perspectives, which shade into each other. Whether we are faced with a performance or a text, reality is formed and re-formed in an open-ended process of interpretation.

Reading and writing

As the example of 'In the Gallery' shows, the texts written in 1916–17 have an experimental, self-reflexive dimension. Several stories thematize the dynamics of interpretation and the relationship between author, text and reader – not as their main theme, but indirectly.

'An Ancient Manuscript' ('Ein altes Blatt') revisits some of the issues raised in Kafka's animal stories. A cobbler recounts how his city – the capital and residence of the Emperor – is invaded by armed nomads from the north. These intruders set up camp in the square outside the palace, sullying the streets and depleting the local food supplies. No one knows where they have come from, and it is impossible to communicate with them as they do not speak the local language. Indeed, they seem barely able to talk at all: 'Among themselves they communicate rather like jackdaws. One hears this jackdaw's cry constantly.

Their incomprehension of our way of life, our institutions, is on a par with their indifference to them. Consequently they respond to any kind of sign language by rejecting it' (*HA* 19/*DL* 264–5). Whereas Kafka's animals are often strangely human, these nomads resemble wild animals. Their speech sounds like the cries of jackdaws, and they also show a strange affinity with their horses. Disturbingly, both riders and horses are carnivores, and sometimes both can be seen feasting on the same piece of meat. Once the nomads are given a living ox, which they devour alive, tearing pieces from the screaming animal. This scene marks the text's gruesome climax; it recalls the ending of 'Jackals and Arabs', where the jackals tear into a camel's still-warm carcass, but this passage is more disturbing and violent. The nomads' behaviour underlines a recurring theme in Kafka's animal stories: violence and savagery are by no means limited to the animal kingdom, but are an intrinsic part of humanity.

The first-person narrator describes these unsettling events, but he also tries to understand the origins of the current crisis. By way of an introduction, he notes, 'It is as if the defence of our country had been much neglected. We have not been worried about it until now ... however, recent events have given us cause for concern' (*HA* 19/*DL* 263). This criticism becomes more explicit towards the end, when the narrator points out that 'the Imperial Palace has attracted the nomads here, but doesn't know how to drive them away again' (*HA* 20/*DL* 266). Having failed to defend the country against this invasion, guards and Emperor have barricaded themselves inside the palace, leaving 'the salvation of our country' to the local people; 'but we are not up to such a task; and we have never boasted that we were capable of it, either. It is a misunderstanding; and it will be our ruin' (*HA* 20/*DL* 266–7).

The story was written in February or March 1917, a few months after the death of Austrian Emperor Franz Josef I, who had reigned for almost sixty-eight years. He was succeeded by his grand-nephew Karl, who reigned only until the end of the First World War, which spelled the end of the Habsburg monarchy. Although the Emperor in Kafka's story is not actually dead, the text nonetheless echoes the Austrian situation in 1917. It depicts a country at war, abandoned by the very sovereign who had brought about this crisis.

The story's title, 'An Ancient Manuscript', is really a meta-title. It refers not to the recounted events but to the text as text, that is, to the medium on which these events are recorded. The age of this manuscript implies that the recorded events took place a long time ago, while the fact that we are dealing with '*An Ancient Manuscript*' – the German '*Ein altes Blatt*' literally means 'an old page' – suggests a sense of incompleteness. In Kafka's notebook, the story is followed by a postscript, the comment of a fictional editor: 'This (perhaps all too Europeanizing) translation of a few old Chinese manuscript pages has been made available to us by a friend of the "campaign". It is a fragment. There is no hope that the remainder might be found' (*NS I* 361). This postscript raises further doubts about the text's reliability. The translation may well be inaccurate, and the text itself is incomplete, for it describes the beginning of the occupation but not its further development and potential conclusion. Just as the narrator cannot understand the nomads' language, so we as readers are unable to read the original, which would in any case be incomplete. 'An Ancient Manuscript' thus points to a more general, recurring issue in Kafka's writings: the difficulty of interpretation, which is exacerbated by unreliable narrators and translators, by cultural difference and the physical fragility of the text.

The short text 'A Message from the Emperor' ('Eine kaiserliche Botschaft') is concerned with similar problems of communication, but harks back to an even earlier stage in human civilization: the oral transmission of messages and stories.

On his deathbed, the Emperor sends out a message to one of his subjects: 'to you, the solitary, the miserable subject, the infinitesimal shadow who fled the imperial sun to far and furthest parts, to you and none other, the Emperor from his deathbed has sent a message' (*HA* 28/*DL* 280–1). Rather than entrusting his missive to paper, the Emperor whispers it into the ear of a messenger. Although the messenger is strong, his progress fast and unimpeded, the distance he has to cross is so great that he will never reach his destination. Each seemingly endless stage of his journey leads on to another, even vaster, space to be crossed, 'and so on through the millennia' (*HA* 28/*DL* 281–2). As the text concludes, 'No one will get through here – and certainly not with a message from the dead. – You, though, will sit at your window and dream it up for yourself, as evening falls' (*HA* 28/*DL* 282).

Kafka's story can be read as a parable about textual interpretation. In such a reading, the Emperor embodies the author who, according to a traditional, hermeneutic model of literary criticism, dispatches his messenger – the text – to communicate a particular meaning to the reader. In Kafka's text, however, this straightforward process is put into question. The 'author' is dying and his messenger unable to convey his message. This situation in turn puts the onus on the reader (the 'you'), who is no longer just the passive recipient of textual meaning but has to take charge of its production. As the French critic Roland Barthes put it fifty years later, 'The birth of the reader must be at the cost of the death of the Author.'[12]

Underlying Kafka's writings is a crisis of communication: the unreliability of media *and* messengers which obscure what they are meant to record and transmit. This worry is particularly pronounced in Kafka's love letters, where he anticipates – or arguably creates – all sorts of misunderstandings. His prose works are based on a more egalitarian, dialogical relationship between writer and reader. The readers of his texts are free – or perhaps compelled – to participate in the production of meaning.

Responsibility

Kafka's texts up to *The Trial* focus on the experiences of the sons. Their protagonists are crushed by the authority of literal or metaphorical father figures, by the destructive power wielded by individuals and institutions. One story from the *Country Doctor* period that harks back to this narrative pattern is the posthumously published fragment 'The Knock at the Courtyard Gate' ('Der Schlag ans Hoftor'). The first-person narrator is arrested after his sister absentmindedly knocks against a manor gate. The stark discrepancy between 'crime' and punishment is reminiscent of Kafka's earlier texts, as is the merciless efficiency of the ensuing process. On the whole, however, 'The Knock at the Courtyard Gate' is rather atypical of the stories written in 1916–17. The emperors of 'A Message from the Emperor' and 'An Ancient Manuscript' are fading patriarchs, unable to exercise their authority. In this, they are complemented by two literal fathers. Both 'Eleven Sons' ('Elf Söhne') and 'Odradek, or Cares of a Householder' ('Die Sorge des Hausvaters') are narrated by father-figures; as we are given insights into their mindset, however, we quickly realize that the father's role is far from easy. It comes with its own burdens, including the burden of responsibility, which they share with other characters such as the eponymous country doctor.

'Eleven Sons' is a strangely uneventful text, barely a story. The narrator describes his eleven sons one by one, but the result is not very cheering. In some cases, the father's account is positive at first but then gets overshadowed by misgivings, while in others he is damning but then finds some redeeming features. The overall impression is one of deep ambivalence, of a father unable to put aside his own reservations and those of others. The effects of this merciless scrutiny can be seen in the text. The narrator starts with the proud statement 'I have eleven sons' (*HA* 30/*DL* 284), but the closing sentence is much more detached: 'These are the eleven sons' (*HA* 34/*DL* 292). By describing his sons to himself and the world, the narrator is left feeling alienated and uncertain.

Something similar happens in 'Odradek, or Cares of a Householder', one of Kafka's strangest and most fascinating stories. The narrator, the 'Householder' or, literally, the 'House Father' (*Hausvater*), of the title, describes his relationship to a creature which occasionally dwells in his home. 'Eleven Sons' starts in a familiar tone and ends on a more distant note, but here the reverse is the case. The first three paragraphs read more like an academic treatise than like a story. We are initially offered an etymological debate surrounding the word 'Odradek', a word whose meaning or derivation cannot be satisfactorily established. This linguistic discussion is then given a more concrete basis in the second and third paragraphs, which describe the 'being' bearing this name. The German term *Wesen* ('being'), suggests a living creature, but at first sight Odradek seems to be a thing, a kind of cotton reel on two legs. It is only in the fourth paragraph that the neuter pronoun 'it' turns into 'he' as Odradek is revealed to be a moving creature with whom the narrator has brief and rather fruitless conversations. Sometimes Odradek responds to questions, but often he is silent 'like the wood that he seems to be made of' (*HA* 29/*DL* 284).

Towards the end, the text gives us an insight into the narrator's mind. Because of Odradek's smallness, the narrator is tempted to treat him 'like a child', but this paternal attitude is mixed with more negative emotions. 'Is it possible for him to die?' he wonders, but just as Odradek seems to have no particular purpose, he does not seem to age or decay. In fact, the narrator imagines that Odradek might still roam the house among his own 'children or grandchildren'; as he admits, 'the idea that he should outlive me does almost give me pain' (*HA* 29/*DL* 284). Situated between living creature and dead object, Odradek embodies the limits of human understanding and indeed of human life itself. He who cannot die confronts the narrator with his own mortality.

Kafka dedicated the *Country Doctor* collection to his father – less, perhaps, to win his approval than as an acknowledgement to himself that our upbringing, however restrictive, shapes our identity and imagination. Yet Kafka's collection takes the family narrative in new directions. 'A Report to an Academy' describes the experiment of socialization outside the family, while 'Odradek, or Cares of a Householder' offers yet another alternative to biological lineage. Odradek is a non-human adjunct to the family, a thing-creature of uncertain origins. Through etymology, the narrator tries to construct for him a substitute lineage, but Odradek resists these attempts, challenging the role of the father as the name-giver, the creator of identity.

The effects of this are both liberating and unsettling. Kafka compared writing 'The Judgement' to the act of giving birth, but in the *Country Doctor* collection he turns from a maternal to a paternal model of authorship. Both 'Eleven Sons' and 'Odradek, or Cares of a Householder' can be read as texts about the writer's predicament. Like the father in 'Eleven Sons', Kafka had very mixed feelings towards his literary 'offspring' and found fault with almost all his texts. 'Odradek, or Cares of a Householder' takes this analogy a step further.

The narrator claims that Odradek 'appears meaningless, but in its way complete' – a statement which can be applied to many of Kafka's short stories, which are tightly structured yet opaque. But if Odradek is the embodiment of the literary text, the householder's concerns about the future gain an autobiographical, self-reflexive dimension. In 1921, Kafka instructed Max Brod to destroy all his unpublished manuscripts, letters and diaries after his death; this order, which Brod disobeyed, betrays Kafka's own anxiety – that his texts, like estranged children, would outlive him, would have an afterlife beyond their creator's control.

Another opaque text is the collection's title story, 'A Country Doctor'. Its eponymous protagonist is called to see a patient, but as the story unfolds he falls short of his role as a figure of reason and responsibility. In this respect, Kafka's text resembles other modernist works, such as Robert Wiene's silent movie classic *The Cabinet of Dr Caligari* (1920) and Arthur Schnitzler's *Dream Story* (1926), in which doctors fall prey to dark desires. The narrative consists of a string of strange events, which unfold in an associative, unpredictable manner. Perception is shot through with fantasy, and actions are motivated not by rational considerations but by darker impulses of aggression, guilt and desire. The text is written without paragraph breaks, in a fluid, breathless narration punctuated by recurring motifs.

In a famous statement, Freud proclaimed that the ego 'is not even master in its own house'.[13] The house becomes the metaphorical site of conflicts within the self, and Kafka's texts often use space in a similar way. The eponymous country doctor needs to answer a nocturnal call, but his horse has died in the harsh winter. When he absent-mindedly kicks open the door of an old pigsty, he discovers to his surprise a groom and a pair of strapping horses. The pigsty is reminiscent of the lumber-room in *The Trial*; both are unused, squalid spaces, which confront the protagonist with disavowed desires. Groom and horses have been interpreted as embodiments of the doctor's libidinous drives, which he has to stifle in order to fulfil his professional duty, but the distinction between groom and doctor – in Freudian terms, between id and ego – remains blurred. As the doctor is pulled away, the groom pursues Rosa the maid into the house:

> I can hear the chain on the door rattling as she fastens it; I can hear the
> lock engaging; I can see how she is putting out the light in the hall,
> and running on through the rooms putting out all the other lights too, to
> make it impossible to find her ... I can still hear the sound as the
> door to my house bursts open and splinters under the groom's onslaught;
> then a roaring fills my eyes and ears, assailing all my senses with equal
> intensity.   (*HA* 14/*DL* 254–5)

The doctor witnesses these events in dreamlike intensity; he is both the fleeing maid protecting her virtue and her determined pursuer. Revealingly, it is only after the groom declares that he will stay at home with Rosa that the doctor himself starts using her proper name, and he later thinks of her as 'that lovely girl, who has for years been living in my house while I have scarcely noticed her' (*HA* 15/*DL* 257).

This pattern, whereby something vital goes at first unnoticed, recurs during the doctor's consultation. On first examination, he judges his patient, a young boy, to be perfectly healthy, and it is only when he looks again, prompted by the subtle clue of 'a badly blood-soaked towel' (*HA* 15/*DL* 257–8), that he discovers a large, festering wound. 'Rose-red in many shades, dark in the depths, growing light towards the margins', it is filled with worms 'as thick and long as my little finger' (*HA* 16/*DL* 258). The wound has obscene, genital overtones; it is located 'in the region of the hips', and the worms wriggling around in it evoke both copulation and decay.

The wound, at first invisible and then hyper-vivid, defies the conventions of realism, and the boy's response is equally contradictory. When the doctor first examines him, he whispers to him, 'Doctor, let me die' (*HA* 14/*DL* 255), but after his wound has been diagnosed, he asks, crying, 'Will you save me?' (*HA* 16/*DL* 258). However, the discovery of the wound also changes the behaviour of the rest of the family. Having previously treated the doctor with great respect, they now force him to take part in a strange ritual. They undress him and put him in bed with his patient, chanting:

> Strip him of his clothes, and then he'll heal you,
> And if he doesn't heal you, kill him!
> He's just a doctor, just a doctor. (*HA* 16/*DL* 259)

Like many of Kafka's texts, 'A Country Doctor' is set in a no-man's-land between tradition and modernity. In the secular age religion has lost its purpose; the village priest sits at home as the villagers have abandoned 'their old faith' (*HA* 16/*DL* 259), but this does not spell the dawn of a new rational era. By the end of the story, the doctor has been stripped of his professional authority and his personal dignity. After an enigmatic conversation with the dying boy, he escapes through the window naked, throwing his clothes into the carriage. As he sets off, his fur coat is out of his reach, and the once miraculously fast horses are dragging along 'like old men' (*HA* 17/*DL* 261).

Nakedness in Kafka's texts is not a return to a more 'natural' bodily state but a sign of humiliation, a harbinger of death. Both prisoner and officer in 'In the Penal Colony' are naked when they are put under the machine, and Josef K. strips down to the waist for his execution. The conclusion of 'A Country Doctor' is less violent but no less chilling. Here the prospect is not death but an endless, meandering journey. In this, the country doctor resembles the huntsman Gracchus, one of Kafka's most mysterious characters, who after his death is forced forever to travel the seas, trapped in limbo between life and death.

At the end of the story the doctor gloomily revisits the preceding events:

> my flourishing practice is lost; a successor is stealing from me, but to no avail, for he can't replace me; that foul groom is running wild in my house; Rosa is his victim .... Deceived! Deceived! Once you have been led astray by the sound of the night-bell, it can never be put right.   (*HA* 17–18/*DL* 261)

As so often in Kafka's writings, a minor event can have vast consequences. But why does the doctor claim that he was 'led astray' by the ringing of the night bell? The boy did turn out to be ill, even though the doctor could not help him; arguably, though, the doctor's conclusion refers not simply to this particular call but to his call*ing* more generally.

Kafka had initially planned to give his volume *A Country Doctor* the title 'Verantwortung' ('responsibility'). In the end he named the book after its most enigmatic story, but responsibility is one of the central concerns in the collection, where various characters – such as the Emperor in 'An Ancient Manuscript', the traveller in 'Jackals and Arabs' and the witness Pallas in 'A Brother's Murder' ('Ein Brudermord') – fail to take responsibility and instead let events run their course. The title story offers an even bleaker conclusion, for even when someone *is* willing to rise to the challenge, he finds it impossible to succeed. The 'Country Doctor' story thus points to a more general crisis of responsibility, which is also a crisis of authority, of vocation and communication. In German, the prefix *ver-* often implies a sense of failure, of an action that has gone wrong. Thus the German word for responsibility, *Ver-antwortung*, implies a failed answer or response (*Antwort*): a scenario of miscommunication. This is borne out in Kafka's title story. If the call that summons the doctor to fulfill his duty leads him astray, the very foundations of responsibility, which are also the foundations of community, are thrown into crisis. As we shall see, the precarious relationship between individual and community remains a central theme in Kafka's late writings.

The Castle

An insomniac novel

From 1910 onwards, Kafka wrote mainly at night. For him the night was a time of inspiration, of complete, trance-like immersion, but this writing strategy also came at a price. In October 1911, Kafka notes in his diary,

> I believe this sleeplessness comes only because I write. For no matter how
> little and how badly I write, I am still made sensitive by these little
> agitations . . . and, in the general noise that is within me and which I have
> no time to command, find no rest.   (2 October 1911; *D* 61/*TB* 51)

Kafka went through long patches of sleeplessness, exacerbated by his extreme
noise sensitivity, and while writing and insomnia did at times form a creative
partnership, sleeplessness could also seriously impede literary production.
After he was diagnosed with tuberculosis in 1917, his insomnia worsened,
and in January 1922 he suffered a nervous breakdown. He was granted leave
from work, which he spent in a sanatorium in Spindelmühle in the Tatra
Mountains. This change of location had a positive effect, for around this time
he embarked on *The Castle* (*Das Schloss*), his third and final novel. *The Castle* is
Kafka's longest text, and he kept working on it until the end of August 1922,
when he suffered another insomnia-induced breakdown.

Work on *The Castle* is thus framed by insomnia at either end, and this
experience also permeates the novel, its characters, style and perspective.
Kafka's protagonist, K., does not get much sleep. A stranger in the village, he
does not have his own bed, let alone his own room, but is forced to sleep on
floors, in armchairs and in other people's beds. As K. becomes more and more
tired, he acts increasingly erratically; towards the end of the novel he misses a
unique opportunity when he falls asleep in the middle of a conversation. K.'s
sleeplessness thus contributes to the novel's narrative tension, and it also underpins the shape and structure of the text. The world of *The Castle* is seen as if
through tired, sleepy eyes. Certain details stand out in almost excessive clarity,
but elsewhere spatial boundaries are blurred, and characters merge into one
another, resembling each other in either name or appearance. The wintry setting
contributes to this sense of disorientation; the snow covers everything, turning
castle and village into an amorphous space without clear outlines.

Routes into *The Castle*

The opening of *The Castle* is surrounded by an air of mystery and uncertainty:

> It was late evening when K. arrived. The village lay deep in snow. There
> was nothing to be seen of Castle Mount, for mist and darkness sur-
> rounded it, and not the faintest glimmer of light showed where the great
> castle lay. K. stood on the wooden bridge leading from the road to the
> village for a long time, looking at what seemed to be a void.   (*C* 5/*S* 7)

The novel is probably set somewhere in Europe, but its precise location is never
spelled out, and this is complemented by the protagonist's truncated name and

unknown origins. The wintry setting adds to the sense of remoteness and isolation; with the castle looming above the village, it is reminiscent of gothic novels such as Bram Stoker's *Dracula*, which are set in equally hostile terrain. Kafka's previous two novels end (or trail off) with the protagonist entering an inhospitable landscape; both the dark mountain range in *The Man who Disappeared* and the quarry in *The Trial* are harbingers of death. In *The Castle*, K. emerges from such an inhospitable landscape into the world of the village, but while its houses offer shelter against the elements, nature nonetheless remains omnipresent through the cold, the early nightfall and the snow that impedes K.'s every step.

On K.'s arrival, darkness, snow and fog combine to hide the castle from view, and the narrative adds to this sense of uncertainty. We are told that not even the faintest glimmer of light is emanating from the castle, and yet K. spends a long time looking up into 'what seemed to be a void', a behaviour which implies that he knows about the castle's existence and location. What is more, in this very sentence which emphasizes the castle's invisibility, the castle is described as *groß* – 'big' or 'great'. From the outset, then, the narrative revolves around a gulf between seeing and knowing. Is this reference to the 'great' castle uttered by an omniscient narrator who imparts his knowledge to the reader, or does this reflect K.'s own perspective, the fact that he comes armed with prior knowledge about the castle? This question is never answered. The following morning, the darkness and fog have lifted, but the extent of K.'s knowledge as well as the motives behind his journey remain shrouded in mystery.

The Castle tells the story of an arrival – a classic route into a narrative – but then K. pauses, hovering on the threshold of his new life. The same hesitation informs Kafka's writing strategy. His notebook contains not one but two openings in immediate succession; the beginning of the novel as we know it is preceded by a fragment describing the arrival of a stranger in a village: 'The landlord greeted the guest' (*SA* 115). This nameless guest is shown into the 'prince's room'; having just arrived, he immediately threatens to leave again, but the chambermaid begs him to stay. K., in contrast, is offered no bed but lies down in a corner of the taproom, and shortly after he has fallen asleep, he is woken again by the castle warden's son, who questions his right to stay in the village. Thus the two versions unfold in rather different ways, but there are also similarities. In the fragment, the guest tells the chambermaid: 'I am here to battle, but I don't want to be attacked before my arrival' (*SA* 116). K.'s actions betray a similar sense of antagonism towards the castle authorities, but also a desire to be validated by them and accepted into the village community.

The Castle is the first literary project that Kafka undertook after a pause of over two years, and the two different routes into the novel reflect his difficulty of starting afresh. The first version breaks off after a couple of pages; after drawing a horizontal line, Kafka tries again. The second opening has more narrative potential; even once the novel has got going, though, the narrative does not progress in a conventional way but remains stagnant, repetitive and circular. *The Castle* is a novel of attempted beginnings, of a protagonist whose new life never really gets started, for none of the routes he pursues leads anywhere.

K. and the castle

In contrast to the urban settings of Kafka's previous novels, the world of *The Castle* seems timeless, even archaic. The novel depicts a community governed by draconian rules and rigid hierarchies. In fact, however, *The Castle* is a hybrid novel, which fuses tradition and modernity. Old-fashioned modes of transport and traditional trades such as tanner, cobbler and waggoner exist alongside modern technology, for details such as electric light, photographs and telephones firmly place the novel in the modern age. This mix of the old and the new is most evocatively embodied in the castle itself. When Kafka wrote his novel, the monarchies of Germany and his native Austria had been replaced by democracies. The remnant of a bygone era, the castle is home to a modern bureaucratic apparatus, but its administrative procedures are shot through with the residues of an older, feudal world order.

The villagers treat the castle officials with great reverence, declaring them to be unfit for ordinary human contact. Like a religious authority, moreover, the castle shapes rules of human behaviour and interaction. Thus Amalia and her family are ostracized by the villagers after she rejects the advances of the official Sortini. The castle officials are by no means models of moral conduct but use their power to exploit others; crucially, though, this power relies on the villagers' active compliance. Amalia aside, the women in the village seem content and even honoured to sleep with the secretaries; what is more, Amalia's punishment, the exclusion of her family from the community, is not actually ordered by the castle but is inferred and implemented by the villagers, who take it upon themselves to uphold what they regard as the castle laws.

Into this feudal world enters K., the stranger. Compared with the villagers, K. is in many ways a rationalist. He looks at village customs and castle procedures from a detached perspective, criticizing them as arbitrary and absurd. Yet K.'s outsider status is both a strength and a weakness, his attitude towards the castle deeply contradictory. While he refuses to comply with some of its procedures, this does not deter him from his overall goal: to gain access to the castle, or at least to be acknowledged, validated by this institution.

In the course of the novel, K. adopts various guises. During a phone call to the castle he claims to be his own assistant, Josef, while later on he takes on the post of caretaker in the village school. But the most important, as well as the most contested, role to which he aspires is that of land surveyor. Upon his arrival, he claims to have been appointed by the castle in this capacity, but this claim is never verified. K.'s original summons (if it existed in the first place) needs to be confirmed by the castle, but the longer he persists with his efforts, the more obstacles he encounters.

This becomes clear in his conversation with the village mayor. He tells K. the story behind his alleged appointment, a convoluted tale of lost files and miscommunication. At the start of their conversation, K. 'felt how very easy it was to communicate with the authorities. They would bear absolutely any burden, you could hand them anything to deal with and remain unaffected and free yourself' (*C* 55/*S* 94–5) – but this sense of lightness is deceptive, even treacherous. In a pattern which recalls Josef K.'s dealings with the court, the castle seems willing to go along with K.'s claims up to a point, but on closer inspection this compliance turns out to be worthless, an illusion. Thus the village mayor tells K. that Klamm's first letter, by which he had put so much store, 'is not an official communication at all, but a private letter' (*C* 65/*S* 114), and thus does not constitute an official appointment. The phone call to the castle, in which K.'s role is confirmed by the deputy warden Fritz, is equally worthless, for

> There is no telephone connection to the castle ... if we call someone
> in the castle from here, the telephones ring in all the lower
> departments ... Now and then a tired official feels the need to amuse
> himself a little ... and switches the sound back on, and then we get
> an answer, but an answer that is only a joke.   (*C* 66–7/*S* 116)

Underlying these examples is a theme that also features in Kafka's *Country Doctor* collection: a fundamental mistrust in media and communication. Letters, files and phone calls convey no real information, and even face-to-face conversations are likely to be misleading.

This bureaucratic maze should not distract us from a more basic question: what sort of position is it that K. is after, and is he in fact suited to this role? Land surveying involves the mapping out of the physical environment as well as the potential (re-)drawing of boundaries. This can have different effects. In the age of colonialism, foreign lands were surveyed in order to be incorporated into the territory of a colonial power; however, land surveying can also overthrow existing power relations, as was the case after the First World War, when the map of Europe was redrawn and various parts of the Habsburg Empire, such as Hungary and Czechoslovakia, became independent nation states. Revealingly, the village mayor rejects the need for such an appointment:

> You have been engaged, you say, as a land surveyor, but unfortunately we don't need a land surveyor ... The boundary markings of our little farms are all established, everything has been duly recorded. Property hardly ever changes hands, and we settle any little arguments about the boundaries ourselves. (*C* 55/*S* 95)

As the mayor has to admit, however, not all villagers agree with this viewpoint. As land surveyor, K. might have no purpose but to uphold the status quo, but his appointment could also overthrow existing power relations, spelling the dawn of a new, more progressive era.

Arguably, these are futile speculations, for K. never gets to practise his profession. His assistants who, as he claims, are following him with his instruments, never arrive, but are replaced by a buffoonish pair sent by the castle. K. thus lacks both the tools and the manpower to carry out his job but, more importantly, he himself seems ill-suited to his profession. He keeps getting lost in the village and never even manages to get close to the castle mount from where he would be able to survey his surroundings.

Most important of all, the castle itself seems to resist being measured and mapped out. On the morning after K.'s arrival the sun is out and the castle is clearly visible above the village. However, the longer K. keeps looking, the more uncertain he becomes about the precise nature of this building. It seems to him that the castle is 'neither an old knightly castle ... nor a showy new structure' but merely 'a poor kind of collection of cottages assembled into a little town, and distinguished only by the fact that, while it might all be built of stone, the paint had flaked off long ago, and the stone itself seemed to be crumbling away'; in fact, 'if you hadn't known it was a castle you might have taken it for a small town' (*C* 11/*S* 17). K. has come to the village to gain access to the castle, but if the castle is just made up of village houses, K.'s mission, of getting *from* the village *into* the castle, becomes impossible, based on an opposition which does not actually exist.

Encounters

Throughout the novel, K. is the only stranger who sets foot in the village. Soon after his arrival he is brusquely informed by Lasemann that 'hospitality isn't a custom here, and we don't need any visitors' (*C* 15/*S* 24), and the landlady of the Bridge Inn tells K. in no uncertain terms, 'You're not from the castle, you're not from the village, you're nothing. Unfortunately, however, you *are* a stranger, a superfluous person getting in everyone's way' (*C* 46/*S* 80). As a stranger, K. occupies the lowest place in the village hierarchy or, worse, remains excluded from this community altogether. This has knock-on effects on his relationship with the castle. Access to the castle is barred to him as a stranger, and this taboo also extends to contact with the castle officials, who are not able to 'tolerate the sight of a stranger, or not without being prepared for it in advance' (*C* 32/*S* 56).

K.'s non-status as a stranger prevents him from gaining access to the castle, but at the same time it makes acknowledgement by the castle so desirable. In this respect, K.'s story is not all that different from that of Karl Rossmann, another emigrant searching for acceptance and belonging. K. quickly realizes that integration into the village community is an essential step towards acknowledgement by the castle. Indeed, the longer he stays in the village, the harder it is to distinguish between these two goals – if they were ever separate in the first place:

> Only as a village worker . . . could he get anywhere with the castle itself. These villagers, who were still so suspicious of him, would start talking to him once he was, if not their friend, then at least one of them, indistinguishable from, say, Gerstäcker and Lasemann . . . then, he was sure, all paths would be open to him, paths that would have been closed to him for ever, and not only closed but invisible, if it had depended solely on the good graces of the gentlemen up above. (*C* 25/*S* 42)

In spite of his general aloofness, K. makes serious attempts to integrate into the village community, and while he does not make actual friends, he forges several close relationships. *The Castle* features a wide range of secondary characters who appear more rounded and three-dimensional than in Kafka's previous novels. By comparison, K. himself remains rather shadowy and two-dimensional; what we find out about him emerges from his interaction with others, with men, women and children.

Among the men, K.'s closest relationship is with the messenger, Barnabas. When he first meets him, K. is immediately drawn to him: 'His face was clear and open, his eyes very large. His smile was extraordinarily cheering, and although he passed his hand over his face, as if to wipe that smile away, he did not succeed' (*C* 23/*S* 38–9). Barnabas, who is dressed all in white, seems to K. angelic, a kind of epiphany. The Latin *angelus* literally means 'messenger', and Barnabas carries with him a letter from Klamm. But subsequently, Barnabas's aura is gradually dismantled, and the hope that K. has placed in him as his most tangible link to Klamm is sorely disappointed. When K. follows Barnabas, he is led not to the castle but to the small cottage which Barnabas shares with his two sisters and his aged parents. When Barnabas unbuttons his white jacket, he reveals 'a coarse, grubby grey, much-mended shirt over a powerful broad chest like a labourer's' (*C* 30/*S* 52). First impressions are deceptive here, as in other cases. Indeed, K. soon learns from the barmaid Frieda and the Bridge Inn landlady that Barnabas and his family are ostracized from the village community and that by associating with them K. will put himself in the same position.

Undeterred, K. keeps visiting them and has long conversations with Barnabas's sister Olga, who tells him of Amalia's downfall. Another conversation concerns Barnabas and his position. Although he is entrusted with letters and allowed into the castle, he is not officially employed as a messenger, just as his official-looking jacket was homemade before he even started to work for the castle. As Olga says,

> For a long time he'd have liked to have, well, not a livery, because there is no such thing at the castle, but an official suit, and he was promised one too, but they are very dilatory about such things at the castle, and the worst of it is that you never know what the delay means. It could mean that the matter is going through official channels, but then again it could mean that the official process hasn't even begun, that – for instance – they want to test Barnabas more first. And finally, it could also mean that the case has already been through official channels, and Barnabas will never get that suit. Nothing can be discovered in more detail, or only after a long time. (*C* 153/*S* 272–3)

For the time being, then, Barnabas just acts out the role of castle messenger, hoping that his actions will eventually bring about the official appointment. In this, his situation resembles that of K., who clings to the hope of being confirmed as land surveyor. But Barnabas's official status is not the only uncertainty surrounding his role. The secretary from whom he receives his orders may not actually *be* Klamm but might only *look* like Klamm, and the castle offices, which he enters on his errands, might not actually be part of the castle:

> And even if the castle does have offices, are they the offices which Barnabas is allowed to enter? He goes into offices, yes, but that's only a part of the whole, for there are barriers, and yet more offices beyond them ... You mustn't imagine those barriers as distinct dividing-lines; Barnabas always impresses that upon me. There are barriers in the offices that he does enter too; there are barriers that he passes, and they look no different from those that he has never crossed, so it can't be assumed from the outset that beyond those last barriers there are offices of an essentially different kind from those into which Barnabas has been. We think so only in those gloomy hours. (*C* 154–5/*S* 275)

Olga's convoluted explanations recall an earlier passage. Just as the castle complex seemed to be made up of village houses, its internal structure is similarly amorphous. The offices that Barnabas is allowed to enter might be not part of the castle but a kind of barrier, a threshold to be crossed on the way into it, or rather a whole succession of barriers. Ultimately, then, the entire castle might be nothing more than a liminal space, a succession of thresholds with no actual core or interior. Olga's account of Barnabas's connection to the castle throws up doubt upon doubt. Like the barrier, which is not fixed but mobile and continually shifting, the identity of the castle cannot be defined or resolved.

Despite Barnabas's uncertain situation, K. continues to place much hope in him. In contrast, he treats the two assistants who are assigned to him by the castle with aggression and contempt. Their names, Artur and Jeremias, are distinctive enough, but to K. they look identical, although others seem to have no trouble telling them apart. This implies a kind of perceptual defect on K.'s part, an inability to see people as individuals. As he tells them, 'you're as like as two snakes' (C 20/S 33) – a comment which takes away their individuality and humanity.

The assistants are both comical and unsettling, childish yet strangely virile; Frieda speaks of 'the way they'd hop about like children but reach out their arms to me like men' (C 124/S 220). They follow K. wherever he goes and invade even his most intimate moments. K. discovers them in the taproom the morning after his first night with Frieda, and when he and Frieda move into the school, the assistants follow them, turning the couple into a kind of family. While Frieda is mild and lenient, K. is a stern, even violent father-figure. He makes the assistants wait outside in the cold, punches Artur with his fist when he finds him in his bed, and takes with him a 'willow switch' to beat Jeremias when he comes looking for K. at Barnabas's house (C 203/S 365). K. takes the assistants and their loyalty for granted, but in the ensuing conversation the tables are turned. Jeremias tells K. that Frieda has left him because of his closeness to Barnabas and his sisters, and that he and Artur have quit their posts. As K. looks at Jeremias, the assistant suddenly looks different, much older. In fact, K. thinks of him as 'this lump of flesh that sometimes gave the impression of not being properly alive' (C 207/S 371); in this Jeremias is reminiscent of Josef K.'s executioners in The Trial, whose fatness and corpse-like pallor are repulsive as well as unsettling.

Jeremias also reveals that, as assistants, their main instruction from the castle had been to cheer K. up, since he 'takes everything very seriously' (C 204/S 368). This suggests that their silly, childish behaviour has been an act, a performance put on to amuse their master. K. is thrown by this revelation.

Here, as elsewhere in Kafka's texts, characters who had seemed rather two-dimensional – at least in the eyes of the protagonist – suddenly reveal hidden depths, and it is impossible to draw the difference between play-acting and 'serious' behaviour. After their conversation, K. returns to the Castle Inn, confident that he can win back Frieda, but when he gets there he discovers that Jeremias has taken his place as Frieda's lover.

While K. tends to categorize the men he meets in narrow terms, the women in *The Castle* are more complex figures, characterized by a strange mixture of strength and weakness. The matronly landlady spends most of her time in bed, and yet she is a formidable figure who dominates her boyish husband and soon becomes K.'s most powerful enemy. Official positions in the village are held by men such as the village mayor, but women arguably have the greater power, based on personal connections to the castle. Both Frieda and the landlady were Klamm's mistresses, while Frau Brunswick, by whom K. is fascinated when he meets her in Lasemann's house, introduces herself as 'a girl from the castle' (*C* 15/*S* 25). Even Mizzi, the mousy and timid wife of the village mayor, turns out to be more important than her husband.

The main female character in the novel is the barmaid Frieda. She is described as 'a small blonde, rather insignificant, with a sad face and thin cheeks', but her gaze is 'of conscious superiority' (*C* 35/*S* 60–1). K. is immediately attracted to her, and the night they first meet they have sex on the floor underneath the bar in the Castle Inn. K. and Frieda roll around in the beer puddles, oblivious to their surroundings:

> Hours passed as they lay there, hours while they breathed together and their hearts beat in unison, hours in which K. kept feeling that he had lost himself, or was further away in a strange land than anyone had ever been before, a distant country where even the air was unlike the air at home, where you were likely to stifle in the strangeness of it, yet such were its senseless lures that you could only go on, losing your way even more. So it was not a shock to him, at least at first, but a cheering sign of dawn when a voice from Klamm's room called for Frieda in a deep, commanding, but indifferent tone. (*C* 40/*S* 68–9)

This sex scene is full of ambiguity, combining elements of romance and disgust, closeness and alienation. The word *gemeinsam*, 'together', is used twice in this passage, but words based on *fremd*, 'strange' or 'alien', appear three times. Losing himself in Frieda, K. feels that he is getting lost in an unknown territory, that his body is invaded by this strangeness through the air that he breathes. Indeed, within the same sentence, breathing shifts from a sign of unity to an experience of suffocating estrangement.

I mentioned above the novel's two different opening passages, which are recorded in Kafka's notebooks. In fact, however, *The Castle* has not just two but three different beginnings. When Kafka started writing his novel, it was conceived as a first-person narrative. Thus the first lines would have read: 'It was late evening when *I* arrived ... *I* stood on the wooden bridge leading from the road to the village for a long time, looking at what seemed to be a void.' Kafka maintained this first-person narrative up to the point when K. and Frieda have sex; perhaps this moment felt a little too intimate to be recounted in the first person. Once he had made the switch, Kafka went back to the beginning, meticulously changing all verbs and pronouns to the third person, but otherwise he left everything unchanged. Arguably, the greater distance from the protagonist which informs a third-person narrative was already implied in the original version.

This sex scene has far-reaching consequences, both for the novel's narrative perspective and for its plot. Unlike in Kafka's previous novels, sex leads to a serious relationship. K. and Frieda set up home first at the Bridge Inn and then in the village school; they even plan to get married, and Frieda dreams of emigrating to France or Spain, but K. feels unable to leave the village: 'I came to this place meaning to stay here' (*C* 121–2/*S* 215). For K., the stranger, the relationship with Frieda is a way of entering the village community, but it also serves another purpose: to get close to Klamm, the object of his growing obsession.

When they first meet, Frieda reveals that she is Klamm's mistress. As in *The Trial*, the sexual rivalry between men is a central theme, but whereas Josef K. seduced women to get back at the court officials, K.'s motives in *The Castle* are almost the reverse. For him an affair with Frieda is a way of attracting Klamm's attention, of getting closer to him. This plan is spelled out in a passage just preceding their first intercourse:

> K. was thinking more about Klamm than about her. The conquest of
> Frieda required him to change his plans, here he was, getting a powerful
> instrument which might make it unnecessary for him to spend any
> time working in the village.   (*C* 278/*SA* 185)

K. thinks of Frieda not as a person but as a thing, an instrument. This passage shows K. at his most calculating; having spelled out his mindset, however, Kafka subsequently deleted it from the manuscript. K. is not portrayed as entirely cold and heartless; rather, the novel paints a more ambiguous picture of a man torn between reason and emotion, between his plan to gain access to the castle and the desire to forge an existence away from its pervading influence. As he reflects early on in the narrative:

Nowhere before had K. ever seen official duties and life so closely interwoven, so much so that sometimes it almost seemed as if life and official duties had changed places. What was the meaning, for instance, of the power, so far only formal, that Klamm had over K.'s services compared with the power that Klamm really did exert in K.'s bedroom?   (*C* 55/*S* 94)

The power of the castle does not reside in procedures and regulations but in the way it invades the lives of individuals even in their most intimate moments. The dividing line between the public, the official, and the private is repeatedly blurred. K. suffers from this lack of privacy, but when it comes to Klamm, he actively tries to break down this division. As he explains to Frieda,

First I want to see him at close quarters, then I want to hear his voice, and then I want to know from the man himself how he feels about our marriage . . . There could be a good many subjects for discussion, but what matters most to me is to see him face to face . . . But now it's my duty to speak to him as a private person, and as I see it that's much more easily done; I can speak to him as an official only in his office, which may be inaccessible, in the castle or – and I'm not sure about that – at the Castle Inn, but I can speak to him as a private person anywhere, indoors or in the street, wherever I happen to meet him.   (*C* 78/*S* 137–8)

K.'s primary goal is not official acknowledgement by the castle but something more informal and personal. This means seeing Klamm's reaction and hearing his voice – physical contact is supposed to cut through the layers of impersonal communication, of letters, files and phone calls, surrounding the castle.

Despite his repeated efforts, however, K. never actually meets Klamm in person. The closest he gets to this goal is early on, when Frieda allows him to observe the secretary through a peephole in the Castle Inn. Face-to-face encounter is here replaced by one-sided surveillance. Klamm is clearly visible under a bright light bulb and sits completely still, as if posing for a photograph. What K. sees is a paunchy middle-aged man with a moustache, a glass of beer in front of him and a cigar in his hand. But this clichéd image of bourgeois masculinity contains a blind spot. Klamm's eyes are hidden behind his pince-nez, and a little later Frieda casually mentions that Klamm is asleep, a revelation which makes K. exclaim. Why is he so startled by this? Klamm being asleep undercuts even the theoretical possibility that he might be aware of his secret observer. K. craves personal acknowledgement; instead, Klamm's pince-nez reflects his own gaze, his own expectations, back at him.

This sense of rejection is repeated at the end of the chapter 'Waiting for Klamm' ('Das Warten auf Klamm'). Having waited in vain for Klamm to emerge from the Castle Inn, K. looks up at the castle:

> The castle, its outline already beginning to blur, lay there as still as always. K. had never seen the slightest sign of life there. Perhaps it wasn't possible to make anything out from this distance, yet his eyes kept trying and wouldn't accept that it could lie so still. When K. looked at the castle he sometimes thought he saw someone sitting quietly there, looking into space, not lost in thought and thus cut off from everything else, but free and at ease, as if he were alone and no one was observing him. He must notice that he himself was under observation, but that didn't disturb him in the slightest, and indeed – it was hard to tell whether this was cause or effect – the observer's eyes could find nothing to fasten on, and slipped away from the figure.   (*C* 88/*S* 156)

The lifeless castle is anthropomorphized by K., but what he imagines is a figure of inhuman indifference. At stake here is not just a lack of recognition but its conscious refusal. The very thing which K. craves the most is, as he comes to realize, anathema to the castle as the epitome of the modern faceless institution. The same is true of Kafka's other institutions; as the priest says to Josef K., 'The court does not want anything from you. It receives you when you come and dismisses you when you go' (*T* 160/*P* 304). In *The Castle*, this sense of indifference is taken to new levels, for here it is absolute and yet strangely personal. Scenes such as this are among the most unsettling in Kafka's texts, for even open hostility is easier to bear than this vacuum of meaning.

The dangers of autonomy

As we have seen, 'strange' and 'stranger' (*fremd* and *Fremder*) are prominent words in the novel, but they are complemented by a second term which has no direct English equivalent: *Heimat*, meaning 'native country' or 'home', 'in the sense of a place rather than a dwelling'.[14] This word is used at various points in the novel, for instance in the scene where K. and Frieda first make love and where it appears to K. that the air he breathes contains no element of *Heimatluft*, the air of his home town or origins. Here and elsewhere in the novel, *Heimat* becomes a shorthand for what K. has left behind, but also for what he hopes to find in his new surroundings.

This becomes apparent when he first sets eyes on the castle on the morning after his arrival:

> K. thought fleetingly of his own home town, which was hardly inferior to this castle. If he had come here only to see the place, he would have made a long journey for nothing much, and he would have done better to revisit the old home that he hadn't seen for so long.   (*C* 11/*S* 17–18)

As he looks up at the castle, K.'s thoughts are immediately diverted from this sight to the memory of his home town; his quest to enter the castle is ultimately a search for origins. The castle, however, is a poor substitute:

> In his mind, he compared the church tower of his childhood home with the tower up above. The former, tapering into a spire and coming down to a broad, red-tiled roof, was certainly an earthly building – what else can we build? – but it had been erected for a higher purpose than these huddled, low-built houses and made a clearer statement than the dull, workaday world of this place did. The tower up here ... was a simple, round building, partly covered with ivy, and it had small windows, now shining in the sun – there was something crazed about the sight – and was built into the shape of a balcony at the top, with insecure, irregular battlements, crumbling as if drawn by an anxious or careless child's hand as they stood out, zigzag fashion against the blue sky.   (*C* 11/*S* 18)

Even though the church spire is just a human creation, it embodies higher hopes and aspirations which are absent from the castle tower with its irregular, jagged outlines. This sight is associated with both madness and childhood – two states which diverge from the norm of adult rationality. At first sight, K. seems to draw a clear distinction between his old and his new home, but the reference to 'an anxious or careless child's hand' that seems to have drawn the castle turrets suggests that K.'s present experience is infused with childhood fears. In the manuscript, the syntax at this point is on the verge of disintegrating, for the inserted sub-clause 'there was something crazed about the sight' is not separated off with commas or dashes. As K. is overcome by memories, the narrative becomes a stream of consciousness, as 'insecure' and 'irregular' as the outlines of the castle.

The church of K.'s home town is also the subject of a second, more detailed flashback. As he follows Barnabas in the hope of being led to the castle, he recalls a scene from his childhood:

> There was a church in the main square there too, partly surrounded by an old graveyard, which in turn was surrounded by a high wall. Only a few boys had ever climbed that wall, and K. had so far failed to do so. It was not curiosity that made them want to climb it; the graveyard had no secrets from them, and they had often gone into it through the little wrought-iron gate; it was just that they wanted to conquer that

> smooth, high wall. Then one morning – the quiet, empty square was flooded with light; when had K. ever seen it like that before or since? – he succeeded surprisingly easily. He climbed the wall at the first attempt, at a place where he had often failed to get any further before, with a small flag clenched between his teeth. Little stones crumbled and rolled away below him as he reached the top. He rammed the flag into the wall, it flapped in the wind, he looked down and all around him, glancing back over his shoulder at the crosses sunk in the ground. Here and now he was greater than anyone.   (*C* 28–9/*S* 49–50)

What drives the young K. is the desire not to get into the churchyard – which can be entered via the gate – but to survey its crosses sunk in the ground from above. When K. suddenly manages to climb the churchyard wall, this is a moment of almost transcendental triumph, carrying associations of both personal invincibility and a more symbolic victory over death. However, K. does not to leave behind his earthly desires; his ramming the flag into the wall has overtones of sexual aggression, but it is also a colonizing gesture of laying claim to uncharted territory.

This childhood scene anticipates K.'s adult quest to enter, to conquer, the castle, but it also illustrates the futility of this struggle. The boy's triumph does not last, for soon a teacher orders him to climb down again. Obeying him, K. grazes his knee; 'it was only with some difficulty that he got home, but still he had been on top of the wall, and the sense of victory seemed to him, at the time, something to cling to all his life' (*C* 29/*S* 50). While his childhood conquest has stayed with him as a defining moment, this memory might be not a help but a hindrance, the moment of triumph a case of self-deception.

A recurring theme in the novel is freedom, which sums up K.'s struggle for autonomy. Talking to the Bridge Inn landlord, K. declares that he would rather live in the village than in the castle, for 'I prefer to be free at all times' (*C* 9/*S* 14). Here, freedom seems compatible with life in the community, but a little later it is revealed to be an empty, meaningless goal. Having waited in vain for Klamm in the yard of the Castle Inn, K. is left with an ambivalent sensation:

> it seemed to K. as if all contact with him had been cut, and he was freer than ever; he could wait here, in a place usually forbidden to him, as long as he liked, and he also felt as if he had won that freedom with more effort than most people could manage to make, and no one could touch him or drive him away, why, they hardly had a right even to address him; but at the same time … he felt as if there were nothing more meaningless and more desperate than this freedom, this waiting, this invulnerability.   (*C* 95/*S* 169)

This passage replays the childhood scene with inverse conclusions. K.'s 'conquest' of the empty yard is no substitute for the climbing of the wall or indeed for entering the castle, but it harks back to the same underlying aim. Once again, K. has asserted his right to dwell in a forbidden location, and this time no authority figure comes to remove him. As an adult, he seems to have secured the freedom which as a boy he experienced only fleetingly, but once he has reached this goal it turns out to be empty, even desperate. K.'s story is the story of modern man who has freed himself from all dependencies, but struggles to fill this new-found freedom with structure and meaning.

Routes out of *The Castle*

Despite all his efforts, K. never manages to meet Klamm, but towards the end of the novel a different opportunity presents itself. K. has been summoned to the Castle Inn for a nocturnal interview with the secretary Erlanger; overtired, he stumbles into the wrong room and wakes up Bürgel, another secretary. But Bürgel does not seem to mind. On the contrary, he welcomes his unannounced visitor and, in the ensuing conversation, reveals a loophole in the watertight system of the castle administration. If a secretary is caught unawares, in the middle of the night, he will grant his visitor any request, even if it is against the rules, for in this more intimate setting 'one is instinctively inclined to judge things from a more private point of view' (*C* 229/*S* 412).

Although K.'s plan of meeting Klamm in private was unsuccessful, his underlying instinct, as it turns out, was the right one. As a boy, K. suddenly managed to climb the wall with almost dreamlike ease, and here the solution presents itself in an equally dreamlike scene. Bürgel is the fairy who has come to grant the bewitched prince his dearest wish. However, *The Castle* is no fairy tale, and K. is unable to seize this opportunity. Tired and worn out, he can barely stay awake to listen to Bürgel's lengthy elaborations, and the very moment when Bürgel finally gets to the crucial point, K. falls asleep, unable to utter his request. This is a moment of crushing failure, but also of great relief. In his leaden tiredness, it seems to K. that sleep is the goal he has been striving for all along: 'he was not yet deeply immersed in slumber but he had taken the plunge, and no one was going to rob him of that now. And he felt as if he had won a great victory' (*C* 231/*S* 415). K.'s tiredness is thus the symptom of a more fundamental drive or desire: the wish to end his 'dead-tired vigil' (*SA* 403). As W. G. Sebald comments, 'The yearning for peace which in K.'s world only death itself can provide, and the fear of being unable to die ... that yearning, that fear must be reckoned the ultimate motive of K.'s journey to the village whose name we never learn.'[15]

Unlike his namesake Josef K., however, K. in *The Castle* does not die. Just as Kafka experimented with different routes into *The Castle*, he also tried out different routes out of the text. Had K. been awake enough to utter his request, this might have enabled Kafka to end both his novel and his protagonist's struggles. K. falling asleep, on the other hand, reflects Kafka's unwillingness, or inability, to bring *The Castle* to a neat (if sudden) conclusion. Instead, the manuscript ends on a rather different note. As the novel wears on, action is largely supplanted by dialogue. Different characters tell K. their life stories, which in turn are intertwined with those of others, resulting in a rich tapestry of human relations. However, rather than unify these different threads to lead up to a conclusion, Kafka keeps adding new strands and characters. After a long and strangely suggestive conversation about dresses with the landlady of the Castle Inn, who up to this point had only made fleeting appearances, K. goes off to work for the waggoner Gerstäcker, another minor character. In his cottage, he starts a conversation with Gerstäcker's old mother: 'She gave K. her trembling hand and made him sit down beside her. She spoke with difficulty, it was hard to understand her, but what she said' (*C* 275/*S* 495). Here the manuscript of *The Castle* breaks off before we find out what the old woman has to say (see Fig. 5). The novel remains unfinished, and yet its abrupt end reflects a more gradual, ongoing process. In the course of the novel, the pace of *The Castle* progressively slows down as the different narrative threads become increasingly disparate and unmanageable. The old woman's trembling hand and fragile voice mirror the uncertain direction of Kafka's last novel, whose many strands cannot be fused into a conclusion.

'Investigations of a Dog', 'The Burrow', *A Hunger Artist*

In the last years of his life, between 1920 and 1924, Kafka wrote some of his most memorable and intriguing short stories. His health was deteriorating, and these texts are written in a reflexive tone, marking the author's attempt to take stock of his life and work. In this, they continue a process of introspection begun in the so-called 'Zürau aphorisms', which Kafka wrote in 1917–18, after he had been diagnosed with tuberculosis. The aphorisms explore ethical and anthropological issues such as justice, guilt and knowledge in concise but often paradoxical formulations. The stories that Kafka wrote in the 1920s continue this investigation in a different form, for now Kafka returns to narrative to undertake what he calls 'self-biographical investigations'. As he elaborates, 'Not biography, rather investigation and discovery of the smallest components possible' (*NS II* 373). What does Kafka mean by this? His stories of the 1920s

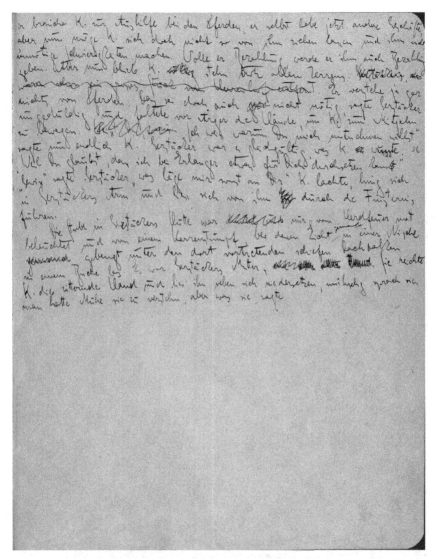

5 The final page of the manuscript of *The Castle*

are no longer concerned with the 'big' issues of the 1910s – family conflict, guilt and punishment, institutions and authority – but focus on more specific concerns: music and silence, food and fasting, childhood and old age. These themes are woven into life stories – stories about outsiders, characters who are fragile, eccentric and often faintly ridiculous. They live on the margins of

6 Passport photo of Kafka (1920)

society, and yet with their strange passions and fruitless investigations, they touch on the very core of human existence.

'Investigations of a Dog'

Several of Kafka's late stories are told by animal narrators, but their premise is rather different from the animal stories of the *Country Doctor* period. No human beings feature in these stories; the world of these animals is self-contained, and while it can be read as an allegory of human existence, it is also distinctly different. Like the ape Rotpeter, the narrators of 'Investigations of a Dog' and 'The Burrow' tell their life stories, but whereas Rotpeter displays a sense of pragmatism, these narrators pursue their projects with a tenacity which borders on obsession and is ultimately self-destructive.

Kafka wrote the fragment 'Investigations of a Dog' ('Forschungen eines Hundes') in 1922, after he had been granted early retirement. Now he was finally free to concentrate on his literary work, but this new freedom, together with his illness, brought various issues into sharp focus. What was the value, the justification of a life dedicated to writing and reflection, especially when contrasted with ordinary, 'productive' forms of existence? Kafka's dog narrator embodies these questions. He looks back over a life dedicated to ultimately fruitless 'investigations'. These investigations were first motivated by his encounter with seven mysterious 'dog-musicians' in his youth, who seemed to produce music out of thin air. This phenomenon leads him to a bigger question: the origins of food and the role of the 'work' the dogs undertake to produce it. A notable exception to this pattern are the 'aerial dogs', who seem to live up in the air 'without showing any visible signs of working at it, but floating at rest' (*HA* 133/*NS II* 447). To investigate the origins of food, the narrator starves himself and almost dies, but he is saved by a 'hunter dog'; following this encounter, he widens his investigation to include the 'music' of the dogs, their 'song', which seems to call down food from the air above (*HA* 151/*NS II* 481).

This seemingly puzzling story follows a simple premise: to the dogs, human beings are invisible. Thus the 'aerial dogs' floating in the air are lapdogs, the 'dog-musicians' circus dogs performing to the sound of music, and the food which magically appears from above is provided by the dogs' human owners.[16] The narrator's investigations are fruitless because they circle around a central blind spot. Kafka's story is an ironic commentary on the search for knowledge, the very nature of intellectual enquiry, but the narrative also touches on social issues. Although his research is meant to benefit the entire dog community, the narrator feels uneasy 'in the middle of the pack's most venerable tribal occasions' and has to admit that in his relationship to his fellow dogs there had long been some little fracture' (*HA* 121/*NS II* 423). The precarious relationship between the individual and the community is a recurring theme in Kafka's late work. The dog's investigations have distanced him from the other dogs, from the life they take for granted. In this respect, he resembles Kafka's artist figures – the hunger artist, the trapeze artist and the mouse singer Josefine, all of whom are dependent on the collective from which they try to set themselves apart.

'The Burrow'

The long fragment 'The Burrow' ('Der Bau') was written in the winter 1923–4, when Kafka was living in Berlin with Dora Diamant. Its narrator is an unspecified animal which lives in an underground burrow. The burrow is the animal's life's work, designed to protect him against enemies; as it turns out, however, this fortress-like structure turns him into a prisoner of his own paranoia. While the 'aerial dogs' floating in mid-air lack a solid foundation, this narrator is buried, incarcerated, and yet his reflections are just as ground-less and futile as those of the dog researcher.

The text falls into two parts. Initially the upkeep of the burrow keeps the narrator busy and relatively content, although every so often he is overcome by sudden tiredness or by uncontrollable bouts of gluttony: 'Happy, but dangerous times! Anyone who knew how to exploit them could, without any danger to themselves, easily destroy me' (*HA* 158/*NS II* 585). Even during these apparently peaceful periods, there is a sense that vigilance can never be sufficient, that any drop in alertness, however brief, might be exploited by potential enemies. In fact, the greater the animal's alertness, the greater the risk of such incidents. Vigilance cannot be upheld indefinitely but is prone to collapse into its opposite, 'total stupefaction' (*HA* 158/*NS II* 585).

Then one day the animal is woken by a hissing sound; after excluding various possible causes, he concludes that this noise must come from another animal, which has invaded his burrow. The narrator searches for this intruder, partly destroying the burrow in the process, but without success: his suspicions are neither assuaged nor confirmed. A closer look at his narrative suggests why this is case. The animal is afraid of outside enemies invading his tunnel, but the most terrifying enemies are those who come from within. Their description is both vivid and vague:

> They are beings within the depths of the earth; not even legend can describe them, even those who become their victims have scarcely seen them;
> they come; you can hear their claws scratching just below you in the earth, which is their element, and already you are lost. (*HA* 154/*NS II* 578)

As readers, we never get an outside view of the narrator, but we know that he himself hunts and kills smaller animals; in fact, this must be exactly how his victims experience his deadly approach. Ultimately, then, the animal's enemy is his double, an outward projection of his own aggression, just as the mysterious hissing might be nothing more than the sound of his own breath. Because of his tuberculosis, Kafka was highly attuned to the hissing, rattling and wheezing which accompanied his every breath. Illness alienates us from our body, turning it into an enemy, an 'other'. Max Brod recalls that Kafka gave a name to his cough: he simply called it 'the animal'.

'The Burrow' is a masterly case study of the psychodynamics of paranoia. If alertness has no outward focus, it turns against itself, creating a target, an enemy, where there is none, without the possibility of either attack or escape. As readers we witness this self-destructive process as it unfolds. The narrative is one long monologue, and the more the story progresses, the more the narrator gets caught up in his own reasoning. Thus, in the second half of the story, the paragraphs get longer and longer, and once the animal has discovered the hissing sound, there are no more paragraph breaks, creating a breathless, labyrinthine narrative with no way out until the narrative breaks off.

A Hunger Artist

In 'The Burrow', the other is a spectre, the product of the lonely narrator's imagination. In *A Hunger Artist* (*Ein Hungerkünstler*, 1924), his last published collection of short stories, Kafka returns to real communities and relationships, but the dynamic between the individual and the community remains deeply precarious. The collection assembles four texts written between 1922 and 1924, and Kafka read the proofs on his deathbed. *A Hunger Artist* is more thematically coherent than Kafka's previous collections, *Meditation* and *A Country Doctor*. Three of the four stories have artists as protagonists; they include the eponymous 'hunger artist', a trapeze artist and a mouse singer. All three protagonists, then, are performance artists; they do not produce artworks that will outlast them, such as paintings, texts or musical compositions; rather, their art is rooted in the present and in the body. Art in Kafka's late stories is not something tangible or permanent, but a process, a state of being, and a dangerous, even lethal undertaking. Indeed, the collection's main theme is not art itself but the artist's existence. Kafka's artists feel isolated and misunderstood, but at the same time they are deeply dependent on their audience, on outside recognition. Their art sets them apart from others, but it is also a form of social interaction.

All three artists have dedicated their lives to their art in ways which echo Kafka's own remarks in his letters and diaries, and yet they are portrayed as ridiculous, even pathetic figures whose art fails to have the intended effect. The tone of these stories is ironic, although this does not preclude a sense of empathy. So are these artists representatives of the author? To read Kafka's late stories as his literary testament, as a kind of personal statement about the purpose of art, would be to miss their point. The stories are full of paradox and ambiguity, and Kafka is at pains to preclude any clear-cut 'message'.

'First Sorrow'

Throughout his life Kafka was fascinated by the circus. He regularly attended circus and variety performances and even read magazines about the circus trade. In his letters and diaries, Kafka repeatedly uses circus imagery as a metaphor for writing. In early 1915, while working on *The Trial* alongside several short stories, he notes: 'Four or five stories now stand on their hind legs in front of me like the horses in front of Schumann, the circus ringmaster, at the beginning of the performance' (18 January 1915; *D* 326/*TB* 718). Here, Kafka uses the imagery of dressage to describe the difficulty of 'taming' the creative inspiration. More often than not, however, he feels that he has failed in this endeavour. A year later he writes to Felice Bauer, 'Am I a circus rider on 2 horses? Alas, I am no rider, but lie prostrate on the ground' (7 October 1916; *LF* 517/*BF* 719–20).

In 'First Sorrow' ('Erstes Leid'), the opening story of *A Hunger Artist*, the focus is not on the circus act itself but on the acrobat's life behind the scenes – although the two cannot really be separated. The first sentence challenges the Romantic ideal of art as a vocation. The trapeze artist practically lives up on his trapeze, 'first out of his striving for perfection and later out of habit turned tyranny' (*HA* 48/*DL* 317). His art, then, is not a calling; it is a habit that has become a compulsion – an idea which will recur later in the collection. The trapeze artist is the most acrobatic and accomplished of Kafka's artists, and his lofty seat is far removed from the drudgery of ordinary life. At this point, however, we might be reminded of a remark by a fellow artiste: the ape Rotpeter in 'A Report to an Academy'. As he argues, the trapeze act, with its apparent suspension of gravity, embodies the human striving for freedom, 'this great feeling of freedom on all sides' (*HA* 40/*DL* 304); to Rotpeter and any ape, however, this human notion of freedom is nothing more than self-deception: 'No building could withstand the laughter of apedom at this sight' (*HA* 41/ *DL* 305). Perhaps such apish laughter would have helped the trapeze artist to escape from his bubble. Instead, he is treated with great reverence, and his every need is attended to. Kafka's texts are full of bad, stuffy air and claustrophobic spaces, but the trapeze artist lives high up in the dome of the circus tent, which is quiet, full of fresh air and flooded with sunlight. When people come up to him, this rarely amounts to real communication; thus the fireman checking the lights calls out 'a few respectful but not very comprehensible words' (*HA* 48/*DL* 318).

The trapeze artist has chosen to keep working 'in the same firm' for the sake of stability (*HA* 48/*DL* 317), but his is a travelling profession, and every so often he needs to move to a new place to give a 'guest performance' (*HA* 49/*DL* 319). This is done by train or even with the help of racing cars, which drive 'through the empty streets . . . at the fastest speed they could' (*HA* 49/*DL* 319). Modern transportation speeds up the trapeze artist's journey, but it also embodies the general instability of modern life. Fortunately, such disruptions are temporary and followed by a period of rest. For the impresario, the artist's paternal friend, it was always the best moment . . . when the trapeze artist set his foot on the rope ladder and in an instant was suspended once more from his trapeze on high' (*HA* 49/*DL* 319).

Up to this point, the narrative mode has been reiterative, describing a recurring pattern. Right at the end of the story, however, one particular incident is recounted in detail. On one of their train journeys, the trapeze artist tells the impresario that he wants a second trapeze; the impresario immediately agrees to this, but the trapeze artist does not seem fully reassured and bursts into tears. After he has fallen asleep in his luggage rack, the impresario watches him and wonders, 'If such thoughts once began to torment him, would they ever completely stop? Could they not but grow in intensity? Were they not a threat to life and livelihood?' (*HA* 50/*DL* 321).

At the end of the story, therefore, a stable situation has become destabilized and is slowly heading towards disaster. This is only a remote prospect – after all, the story is called '*First* Sorrow' – but a prospect nonetheless. Now that the trapeze artist has become dissatisfied with his way of life, no additional bars will ever be enough, and yet he has become so set in his ways that a real change is impossible. The last sentence, then, is only superficially peaceful: 'And the impresario really believed he could see how, at this moment, in the seemingly peaceful sleep in which the weeping had ended, the first furrows began to inscribe themselves on the trapeze artist's smooth and child-like brow' (*HA* 50/*DL* 321).

The case of the trapeze artist echoes Kafka's own, frequently expressed desire for a life free from distractions, a life wholly dedicated to writing. But even if such a life were possible, the text suggests that the true obstacles lie within. 'Only this one bar in my hand – how can I live?' the trapeze artist exclaims at the end (*HA* 50/*DL* 321); the trapeze has been likened to the writer's pen, but both pen and trapeze can become the bars of a cage. By the end, then, freedom has given way to entrapment; curled up in his luggage rack, the trapeze artist resembles the protagonist of 'The Burrow', who keeps expanding his burrow until it has become a prison from which he is unable to escape. No further trapezes can compensate for a lack of human interaction, a lack of groundedness in a community.

'A Hunger Artist'

While 'First Sorrow' ends with a sense of foreboding, in 'A Hunger Artist' decline is a foregone conclusion: 'In recent decades, interest in hunger artists has greatly diminished' (*HA* 56/*DL* 333). After this general statement, the impersonal narrator tells the story of one particular hunger artist, his initial success, descent into obscurity and eventual death. Hunger artists were a common attraction at fairs and in circuses around 1900. Like Kafka's protagonist, they would lock themselves up in a cage and fast for several weeks. Such performances were popular until the First World War, but the war led to famines, and as hunger became a real issue, show fasting lost its popular appeal. In fact, when Kafka was writing the story in 1922, Russia was in the grip of a great famine, and he and his sister Ottla donated money to a relief programme.

In his heyday, the hunger artist was part of the local community. The whole town, including children, took an interest in his fasting; people came to see him on a daily basis, some of them sitting in front of the cage for days on end. But the hunger artist's fasting is hard to grasp. It is based on abstention, on the absence of normal behaviour, and therefore relies on props, helpers and rituals which frame this art, making it visible and comprehensible. The hunger artist's cage contains nothing but a clock and a sign indicating the duration of his fast. In addition, he is supervised around the clock by guards – 'butchers' who do not actually take their role seriously and try to give him the opportunity to eat secretly. These guards do not ensure the authenticity of his art but rather taint and undermine it, and the same is true, in his view, of the time limit imposed on his fasting. His impresario forces the hunger artist to limit his fasting to forty days, reminiscent of Christ's forty-day fast in the desert, arguing that after this point the public will begin to lose interest. The end of the fast is marked by a ceremony, a public meal, but the hunger artist detests all this pomp and tries to stay in his cage to keep on fasting – though without success.

The hunger artist is perhaps Kafka's most sincere and committed artist, and yet he is surrounded by ignorance, by people doubting or spoiling the purity of his art. Although his audience is fascinated by his fasting and his emaciated body, the hunger artist feels that he is the only 'fully satisfied spectator of his own hungering' (*HA* 58/*DL* 337). Ultimately, what the hunger artist is after is fasting without bounds, without limits, an art which exceeds all boundaries and becomes a way of life. In this, he resembles the trapeze artist. Both artists try to overcome the solidity – the gravity – of the human body. Their art is body-art, but their aim is to transform the body, to defy its physical laws and limitations.

In the case of the hunger artist, this total commitment to his art results in self-elimination. Once his popularity starts to decline, he dismisses his impresario and joins a circus. Now that he is no longer forced to stick to a fixed schedule, he can finally realize his dream of fasting without limits. But with hindsight the impresario is proven right. The hunger artist's cage is put up in a busy spot on the way to the stables, and yet he is ignored by most visitors, who believe his fasting to be a sham. The longer he fasts, the more he fades into oblivion, until by the end he has become so thin that he almost disappears underneath the straw.

By choosing the hunger artist as his protagonist, Kafka picks up on a theme that recurs throughout his writings. In an early diary entry, he describes his literary vocation as a process of starvation:

> When it became clear in my organism that writing was the most productive direction for my being to take, everything rushed in that direction and left empty all those abilities which were directed towards the joys of sex, eating, drinking, philosophical reflection and above all music. I atrophied in all these directions. This was necessary because the totality of my strengths was so slight that only collectively could they even halfway serve the purpose of my writing. (3 January 1912; *D* 163/*TB* 341)

Artistic vocation requires complete self-abnegation, the ascetic rejection of all worldly pleasures. Writing is incompatible with consumption – of food, music, other bodies – because it is itself all-consuming. That said, in a characteristic twist, Kafka adds, 'Naturally, I did not find this purpose independently and consciously; it found itself.' To be an artist is less a choice than an inner necessity, a compulsion passed off as self-control. The same applies to the hunger artist. In his dying moment, he tells his supervisor that he does not deserve admiration, for in fact he starved himself only 'because I could not find the food that was to my taste. If I had found it, believe me, I would not have caused a stir, and would have eaten my fill, like you and everybody else' (*HA* 65/*DL* 349). Here, 'A Hunger Artist' harks back to *The Metamorphosis*. Gregor Samsa initially tucks into the rancid food his sister provides for him, but later on he loses his appetite and eventually dies, his body flat and emaciated. Shortly before his death, as he listens to his sister playing the violin, Gregor feels that this music points the way 'to the unknown nourishment he longed for' (*M* 66/*DL* 185). Starvation, for both characters, is not an end in itself but a quest, a search for something beyond the ordinary. Art and music are signposts in this search, but they are not the ultimate goal, which remains out of reach, beyond language.

Like *The Metamorphosis*, 'A Hunger Artist' ends with a kind of epilogue. After Gregor's death, the Samsas emerge from their flat revitalized and full of optimism; the hunger artist's place in turn is taken by a young panther, which becomes a popular attraction. In both texts, life and vitality succeed frailty, asceticism and death. The panther with his voracious appetite embodies a Darwinist model of existence – the survival of the fittest, those at the top of the food chain. But the animal's true attraction lies elsewhere:

> It lacked for nothing. The keepers did not have to reflect for long about bringing it the sustenance that was to its taste; it didn't even seem to miss its freedom; this noble body, equipped nearly to bursting with all the necessaries, seemed to carry its freedom around with it too; it seemed to have it hidden somewhere in its teeth; and its joy of life came with such fiery breath from its jaws that it wasn't easy for the spectators to resist it.   (*HA* 65/*DL* 349)

While the hunger artist searched in vain for the right food, the panther is free from such longing, free even from the desire for freedom, for he carries his own freedom within him – or so it seems to his human spectators. The verb *scheinen*, 'to seem', features three times in this short passage. Here, as so often, Kafka ends on an ambivalent note. The panther seems the diametric opposite of the hunger artist, and yet his freedom might be no more real than the hunger artist's asceticism – a facade which conceals a more complex reality.

'A Little Woman'

Alongside these two male artists, Kafka's collection also features two female protagonists – a first in his oeuvre. Questions of gender loom large in these texts, which rework some of the gender stereotypes that appear in the earlier works. However, the differences between men and women are outweighed by the similarities between the four protagonists. Both the trapeze artist and the hunger artist are frail and fragile, and they share this fragility with the little woman and the singing mouse, Josefine.

Despite such similarities, the story 'A Little Woman' ('Eine kleine Frau') may seem rather out of place in the collection. Unlike the other three texts, it does not revolve around art but around a personal relationship, or rather a confrontation. An unnamed narrator describes how the 'little woman' of the title is annoyed and tormented by him and his very existence. The reason for this antipathy never becomes clear, and neither does the exact nature of their relationship. The narrator insists that there is no romantic bond between them – in fact, that he barely knows her – and yet his account suggests that they are in almost constant contact. His account is full of reiterative formulations such as 'always' and 'often', which make the text strangely static: 'she is always finding fault with me about something, I always offend her, I vex her at every turn; if you could divide life up into the smallest of small parts, and judge *ex parte* each separate little part separately, every particle of my life would assuredly be a vexation to her' (*HA* 51/*DL* 322). It is difficult to tell where the narrator's account ends and the little woman's complaints begin. The narrator seems a kind of ventriloquist, speaking with the voice of his nemesis.

When reading the story, therefore, we need to read between the lines, to try to distinguish between the narrator's professions of innocence and a different, contrasting attitude which comes through in certain formulations. The text begins in the vaguest of terms: 'She is a little woman' (*HA* 50/*DL* 321). This phrase, which picks up on the title of the story, immediately shapes our perspective. The adjective 'little' may simply be a physical description, but it is also unmistakeably condescending. It lends this woman a childlike, childish, character, making it hard for the reader to take her seriously. Her smallness gives her an air of insignificance, and this is underlined by the indefinite article. She is *a* small woman – one of many, the text suggests. Her physical appearance is similarly non-distinctive. Her hair is 'dull-blond', her dress 'like the colour of wood'. The overall impression is one of blandness, a complete lack of contrast. Or so the narrator suggests. As he says, 'I always see her in the same dress' (*HA* 50/*DL* 321) – though others might get a different perspective. The narrator's account thus highlights the subjectively skewed nature of perception. The little woman is an unsettling presence, but she is also blank canvas, a screen for the narrator's projections. So far, we have implicitly assumed that the narrator is male, although this is not spelled out anywhere in the text. The narrator's denial of a romantic connection between them points in this direction; more importantly, the depiction of the little woman betrays a sense of distance, of fundamental alienation, as well as tapping into various misogynist stereotypes.

In *The Man who Disappeared* and *The Trial*, women are depicted as men's adversaries – cunning, manipulative, irrational and seductive; the female characters in *The Castle* are more rounded and complex, with their own voices and histories, but 'A Little Woman' seems to mark a step back again. Here, various clichés of femininity are trotted out. She is irrational, unpredictable, hysterical and cunning, but also frail, and her fits of anger make her 'pale, bleary-eyed, racked by headaches, and almost incapable of working' (*HA* 51/ *DL* 324). On one level, she remains two-dimensional, as wooden as the colour of her dress, and yet she is endlessly puzzling and occupies the narrator to the point of obsession. In fact, his argument, with its generalizing claims and patronizing overtones, is little more than an attempt to control an uncontrollable situation.

The differences between 'A Little Woman' and Kafka's earlier texts are encapsulated in one detail: the motif of the hand. While Leni in *The Trial* has webbed fingers, the little woman's fingers are equally striking, but for a completely different reason:

> I can only render the impression she makes on me by saying that I have never seen a hand where the fingers are as sharply separated as they are on hers; and yet her hand has no anatomical peculiarity about it whatever; it is a perfectly normal hand.   (*HA* 50/*DL* 322)

In *The Trial*, woman is animal-like, exotic and seductive, but categorizable in her otherness. The little woman, in contrast, is 'perfectly normal', and it is this normality which makes her so unsettling. In this, she resembles Kafka's artists. She is ordinary yet extraordinary – just as Josefine's piping and the hunger artist's fasting set them apart without being anything special.

'A Little Woman' is quite an unnerving text. The narrator's argument is hard to follow, and his claims are often contradicted by counter-claims. The more he reasons, the more dubious he appears. Having stressed his own trustworthiness and good reputation, he casually remarks that 'anyone but myself' might have recognized this woman 'as a clinging vine and would have trampled [her] beneath his boot silently and out of the world's hearing' (*HA* 56/*DL* 332).

None of this reasoning, nor indeed this sudden bout of (imaginary) violence, removes the looming threat posed by the situation. Initially, the story involves just two people, but soon their confrontation draws in the woman's relatives, then an unspecified group of 'spies' or 'tell-tales' (*HA* 52/*DL* 325), and finally the general public. As in *The Trial*, the private has become public, and the narrator's actions are judged by a growing group of witnesses and arbiters. By the end, the narrator alludes to the 'looming decision' (*HA* 55/*DL* 331), although he then berates himself for using such a grand word. What, then, is the solution? The narrator declares that nothing, least of all his suicide, could alleviate the woman's anger. Deferring the decision is a possibility, but this deferral strategy brings its own risks, for the longer the narrator waits, the more apparent his flaws become:

> if someone had a rather wary eye as a boy, no one thinks badly of him for it, it is simply not noticed ... but what is left when he is older are remnants ... each one is under observation, and the wary eye of an ageing man is just that, quite clearly a wary eye, and not hard to detect.   (*HA* 56/*DL* 333)

By the end of the text, then, the narrator seems to have accepted, internalized, the little woman's image of him in the same way that Josef K. comes to accept his execution. There is, however, one possible solution, or rather a way out: 'she has only to make up her mind to forget my existence, which after all I have never forced upon her, nor would I ever do so – and all her suffering would clearly be over' (*HA* 51/*DL* 322–3). Closure cannot be achieved by one particular action or event, but only by a gradual process, a fading into oblivion. As we will see, Kafka's last story, 'Josefine, the Singer' ends on a very similar note.

'Josefine, the Singer or The Mouse-People'

'Josefine, the Singer or The Mouse-People' ('Josefine, die Sängerin oder Das Volk der Mäuse') is the collection's final story, and it draws together several of the themes of the previous texts. An anonymous first-person narrator reflects on his/her relationship to the protagonist, the eponymous Josefine. The text does not spell out the narrator's gender, although several critics have assumed him to be male; for Elizabeth Boa, the narrator displays 'the complacent superiority of a normal male mouse indulgently observing an abnormal female'.[17] In this, the narrator is not alone. He is one of the mouse people and speaks on behalf of the collective. When the story was first published in April 1924 in a Prague newspaper, it was simply called 'Josefine, the Singer'. In May, Kafka decided to add the subtitle. As he noted down on one of the 'conversation sheets' through which he communicated as his tuberculosis became worse, 'Such "or"-titles are admittedly not very pretty but here perhaps it makes particular sense; it resembles a pair of scales' (*DLA* 463). The image of the scales suggests that there are two ways of reading the story: as a tale about an artist, or as a story about her audience, the mouse people. In fact, of course, the text explores the relationship between the two, a relationship which is antagonistic, but also close and caring, even symbiotic.

Like many of Kafka's late stories, 'Josefine' does not have a conventional plot but is one long monologue, a string of labyrinthine and often contradictory reflections. The narrator tries to explain Josefine's art and her relationship to her audience but fails to arrive at any clear conclusions. Every claim is followed by a counter-claim, every finding qualified, nuanced or revoked. This is apparent right from the start. The narrator begins in an assertive tone: 'Our singer is called Josefine. If you haven't heard her, you do not know the power of song' (*HA* 65/*DL* 350). But then doubt begins to creep into his argument:

> Is it in fact song at all? Is it perhaps only piping? And of course we are all familiar with piping; it is our people's real skill, or rather, it is not a skill at

all, but a characteristic expression of our life. We all of us pipe, but truly, nobody thinks of claiming it as an art, we pipe without paying any attention to it, indeed, without noticing, and there are even many among us who have no idea at all that piping is among our distinctive characteristics.   (*HA* 66/*DL* 351–2)

The narrative erodes the distinction between art as 'skill' and as 'expression of our life'. All mice pipe – some of them without even being aware of it – but Josefine has somehow managed to set herself apart from the masses, turning her piping into art. The key to this is performance. The narrator remarks on 'the curious situation that here is someone ceremoniously presenting herself – in order to do nothing different from the usual thing', such as cracking a nut (*HA* 67/*DL* 353). As was suggested by Marcel Duchamp's 'readymade' artwork *Fountain* (1917), an upturned urinal, the right context can turn even something mundane into art – or perhaps reveal that the mundane has been art all along. The boundary between art and non-art is no longer absolute, but can be redrawn depending on the mode of presentation. In this, Josefine's piping resembles the hunger artist's fasting, which likewise needs a stage (or cage) to be marked out as more than a private obsession. This dependence on performance and staging is a potential weakness. Both Josefine and the hunger artist are faced with audiences that are shallow, disrespectful and easily distracted. The hunger artist soon gives up trying to win them over, but Josefine rises to the challenge. As the narrator has to admit, even her critics, who question the value of her art, are won over by her performance: 'being in opposition is only possible at a distance; if you are sitting in front of her, you know: what she is piping here is not piping' (*HA* 67/*DL* 354). In the auratic presence of the performer, all rational doubt dissolves in a bath of emotions: 'We too immerse ourselves in the feeling of the crowd, fervently listening, bodies packed close, hardly daring to breathe' (*HA* 69/*DL* 356).

The mice may be divided about Josefine's art, but they are very different from the hunger artist's fickle crowd. They are one people, united by a common purpose. Like many of Kafka's late stories, 'Josefine' has been read in the light of Kafka's growing interest in Judaism – as an allegory of Jewish life in an increasingly anti-Semitic society. As the narrator suggests, the mice are a vulnerable group, living in constant fear of being attacked by enemies. In this situation Josefine is both a help and a hindrance. When she is ready to sing, she expects her audience to gather, regardless of whether the moment is right. In some cases, her performance leaves the mice open to attacks, and yet her singing also provides them with strength and solidarity. 'It is not so much a song recital as a people's assembly', offering 'one last cup of peace together before the battle' (*HA 71/DL* 361). Finally, her singing also has a symbolic dimension. In its faintness and transience, it reflects the mouse people's precarious situation: 'Josefine's thin piping in the midst of hard decisions is almost like the miserable existence of our people in the midst of the tumult of a hostile world' (*HA 72/DL* 362).

The title of the story is, as mentioned above, two-fold, drawing our attention both to Josefine and to the mouse people. In the German original, Kafka uses the word *Volk*, 'people', for the nation of mice, an emotionally charged term which was subsequently appropriated by the National Socialists and has since become unusable. In Kafka's time, however, in the wake of the political upheavals of the late 1910s and early 1920s, of the Zionist movement and the foundation of new European states such as Czechoslovakia, of which Kafka was now a citizen, national identity was a hotly debated topic. Kafka's last story explores the ideal, but also the challenges, of national unity.

Indeed, the fraught nature of this ideal is embodied in the protagonist. As individuals, the mice are unable to withstand the constant looming danger, but even the collective resilience has its limits: 'sometimes even a thousand shoulders tremble beneath the burden that was only meant for one' (*HA 68/ DL* 356). In such moments, Josefine comes into her own:

> She is ready and waiting, the delicate creature, trembling alarmingly, especially below her breast. It is as if she had concentrated all her energy in her singing; as if everything in her that did not directly serve her singing had been drained of all her energies, almost of every possibility of life; as if she were exposed, abandoned, given over only to the protection of kindly spirits; as if, while she is dwelling enraptured in her song, a cold breath brushing past might kill her.   (*HA 68/DL* 356)

To be an artist is to live in the vicinity of death. All four stories in the *Hunger Artist* collection feature bodies marked by ageing and decline, and yet these stories also point backwards, to the state of childhood. Both the hunger artist and the trapeze artist, whose 'child-like brow' is marred by wrinkles, are dependent on the paternal care of their impresarios, while the 'little' woman is surrounded by an entourage of family members and other guardians. Although Josefine neither fasts nor performs dangerous acrobatics, her body is described as frail and fragile. She is childlike, and we are told that the mouse people care for her like a father for a child. But this relationship is in fact reciprocal, for in her very frailty Josefine also adopts the role of protector: 'Whenever the news is bad ... she will arise at once ... and attempt to survey her flock like a shepherd before the storm' (*HA 71/DL* 360). Here the roles of child and parent – which in Kafka's earlier texts stood for an ultimately immovable hierarchy – are not fixed but fluid. This in turn reflects the precarious role of childhood among the mouse people. Because of their numerous enemies and the vast number of their offspring, the mice have no real youth, indeed 'scarcely even a brief childhood' (*HA* 72/*DL* 363), but as a result, 'a certain surviving, ineradicable childishness pervades our people' (*HA* 73/*DL* 364). And yet, the narrator adds, 'our people are not only childish, they are also to some extent prematurely old' (*HA* 73/*DL* 365). As an artist, Josefine benefits from this paradoxical conflation of childhood and old age. The mice are both too immature and too old to appreciate real music: 'the excitement, the lift to the heart it produces is not fitting to our gravity; wearily we wave it away; we have withdrawn into piping' (*HA* 73/*DL* 365). Josefine's 'art' is modest, inconspicuous, aimed at listeners with a small attention span, but it is also the product of an artist whose own strength and voice are fading. Thus the narrator remarks that while 'a common toiler in the earth' is able to pipe all day, Josefine's own piping is not just ordinary but stands out through its 'delicacy, or thinness' (*HA* 66/*DL* 352).

Writing in the light of death

Of the four protagonists in Kafka's last collection, only the hunger artist actually dies. For the remaining three, there is no definitive end, only a sense of foreboding. In Josefine's case, the text is infused with the prospect, the spectre, of death. Right at the beginning the narrator remarks that 'with her departure music will … disappear from our life' (*HA* 65/*DL* 350), and at the end he concludes, 'But with Josefine, things are bound to go downhill. Soon the time will come when her last peep will sound and fall silent' (*HA* 79/*DL* 376). Indeed, by this point in the story Josefine has disappeared; her fate is uncertain, but the narrator knows that soon she will be forgotten, 'redeemed and transfigured … like all her brethren' (*HA* 80/*DL* 377). Being forgotten might be a fate worse than death, but in the *Hunger Artist* stories this state is associated with a sense of freedom, of release. Thus the narrator of 'A Little Woman' longs to be forgotten by his nemesis, knowing that this would be his only escape. In the case of Josefine, moreover, oblivion becomes synonymous with remembrance, not of her as a person, but of her art. As the narrator remarks, her singing was so faint and fading that it was barely more than a memory, even during her lifetime, but for this very reason it will be remembered: 'in this way it could never be lost' (*HA* 80/*DL* 377).

Despite the narrator's gently mocking tone, Josefine perhaps comes to closest to being a figure of authorial identification. The medium of her art is her voice, a voice which is no different from that of ordinary people, and which is able to express their collective concerns. This marks a great change from Kafka's earlier models of literary vocation, which, as we have seen in Chapter 1, involved asceticism, complete solitude and isolation. In his late writings, Kafka emphasizes the public role of the artist, as a figure at the heart of the community and yet at its margins.

In a short text written in the spring of 1923, Kafka encapsulates this tension:

> There are many here waiting. An immense crowd which loses itself in the dark. What do they want? They are obviously making particular demands. I will listen to the demands and then answer. But I won't go out onto the balcony; I couldn't even if I wanted. In the winter, the balcony door is locked and the key is not to hand. But I won't go up to the window either. I don't want to see anyone, I don't want to get confused by the sight of anyone; at the desk, that's my place, my head in my hands, that's my posture.   (*NS II* 16)

There are not many texts in which Kafka presents his literary vocation on such a grand, public scale, and yet the text is pervaded by an air of melancholy and resignation. The time is winter and the balcony door (like the cellar door in the letter to Felice) is locked – though not, it appears, by the writer. The writer's seclusion is not a choice, but a necessity. Unlike Josefine and her fellow artists, he does not face his audience, does not risk the distraction and disappointment which inevitably spring from such encounters. It is only by staying at his desk, his head buried in his hands, that he can be true to his vocation. His resigned posture mirrors those of many of Kafka's characters. Josefine's head, in contrast, is not bowed but lifted up, thrown back in defiance. None of the artistic personas and voices that Kafka adopts in his late stories *is* Kafka; but both collectively and as individuals they sum up the tensions – between elation and disappointment, the need for solitude and the search for community – which inform Kafka's writings from the beginning right to the very end.

Chapter 4

Scholarship and adaptations

The size of Kafka scholarship is so vast, his influence on the arts and literature so pervasive, that both by far exceed the scope of any overview. By necessity, this chapter will therefore pursue a more selective approach. The first part outlines the main strands of Kafka scholarship in the twentieth and twenty-first centuries, while the second part explores the challenges of 'translating' Kafka's texts into other media through three film adaptations of his novels: Orson Welles's *The Trial* (1962), Jean-Marie Straub and Danièle Huillet's *Class Relations* (1984, based on *The Man who Disappeared*) and Michael Haneke's *The Castle* (1997).

Editions and translations

Any survey of Kafka scholarship is tied up with the complex history of Kafka editions, for the question of what does or does not constitute the 'original' Kafka text remains a thorny one, both for readers of German and, even more so, for those relying on translations.

Only a fraction of Kafka's works appeared during his lifetime, but less than two months after his death, in July 1924, Max Brod signed an agreement to publish a posthumous edition of Kafka's works. In doing so, Brod ignored Kafka's own explicit instructions, which he had spelled out twice, that all his unpublished manuscripts should be destroyed after his death. Kafka readers thus find themselves in the moral dilemma that by reading Kafka's texts – and particularly his private diaries and letters – they violate the author's own express wishes. Brod himself defended his decision by pointing out that he had at the time told Kafka that he would not carry out this task; if Kafka had been serious with his intention, one could argue, he would have found another way of achieving it.

As Kafka's editor, Brod found himself lumbered with a monumental task. The majority of Kafka's prose texts are unfinished, and in many cases the manuscript situation is ambiguous, making it difficult to decide what constitutes the text proper, or in what order its parts should be arranged. This is particularly true of *The Trial*, which appeared in 1925. Here, and elsewhere, Brod took many liberties in his editions. In the case of *The Trial*, he changed the order of chapters and omitted the unfinished sections to give the impression of a polished, complete work; he gave titles to unnamed, unfinished short stories and changed the name of Kafka's first novel from the cryptic *The Man who Disappeared* to the snappier *Amerika*. By doing so, Brod's aim was to present Kafka's works in a coherent, more 'reader-friendly' format, which would ensure the success they deserved. His strategy had the desired result, but soon the flaws of his approach became apparent. A comparison between the first and second editions of *The Trial* (1925 and 1935), for instance, revealed a total of 1,778 unexplained discrepancies, and Brod made extensive changes not only to previously unpublished texts but also to works which Kafka himself had proofread for publication.

In later editions, Brod included fragments and some variants in an appendix, but it was not until the publication of the new Critical Edition (Kritische Ausgabe), which began with *The Castle* in 1982 and is still ongoing, that readers were able to gain full insight into Kafka's working method, his variations and deletions. Even this edition, however, is not uncontested; Kafka's spelling and punctuation have in part been 'normalized', though this was done in line with the old German spelling conventions, which ironically changed halfway through the edition, so that some of Kafka's original spellings would now in fact be in line with the rules. Trying to strike a balance between scholarly presentation and readability, the Critical Edition still relegates most fragments and alternatives to the apparatus, printed in a separate volume, and for the reader having to switch back and forth between volumes it is still difficult to get a complete picture of the shape of the manuscript. A third, ongoing Kafka edition offers an alternative solution. The Historical-Critical Edition (Historisch-Kritische Ausgabe) presents Kafka's manuscripts as scanned facsimiles, with a typed transcript including variants and deletions on the opposite page. Its aim is to present Kafka's writings as closely to the manuscript as possible, and this is also reflected in the physical volumes. Thus the edition of *The Trial* does not present the novel as one book; rather, each chapter takes up one separate, slim volume to reflect the fact that the chapters have survived as bundles of loose pages, each with its own cover page or sleeve.

Given that the precise order of these chapters remains unclear, the reader of this edition can reshuffle them, free to determine their sequence.

If Kafka editions in German remain a complex issue, this situation is exacerbated when it comes to translations. Kafka is one of the most widely translated of all authors, and in English alone his works exist in many different versions. After the Nazis banned Kafka's books, they could appear only outside Germany; at this point his reception become more international, and translations played an important part in this development. Kafka's first translators into English were Edwin and Willa Muir, who had learnt German unsystematically on their travels in the 1920s. They had to rely on Brod's heavily edited editions, and also went along with his religious interpretation, presenting *The Castle* as a modern-day equivalent of *The Pilgrim's Progress* (1678), John Bunyan's great Christian allegory. Since then, Kafka's texts have been re-translated many times, a task helped by the publication of the Critical Edition, although some current translations are still based on Brod's editions. This includes the English edition of the diaries, which is missing various entries, some of them sexually explicit, which were left out by Brod, probably for reasons of delicacy and 'discretion'. The blue octavo-sized notebooks from 1917 onwards have been translated, but the earlier quarto-sized ones are not available in English. In general, English-speaking readers will find it hard to gain a real impression of Kafka's writing strategy, of variants, alterations and deletions contained in the apparatus of the Critical Edition. This is a gap which this Introduction attempts to fill at least in part, by occasionally drawing on material which is absent from the English texts.

The fact that not all of Kafka texts are available in English is one issue; another is the more general difficulty surrounding the task of translation. This is immediately obvious when we compare the many different renderings of titles and proper names in different translations. Part of the ambiguity of Kafka's texts stems from the fact that he often uses multivalent words; thus *Process* in German means not only 'trial', but also 'process' or 'procedure', while *Schloss* means 'lock' as well as 'castle'. A notorious example is the word used to describe Gregor Samsa in *The Metamorphosis*; the German phrase 'ein ungeheures Ungeziefer' has been translated as 'a monstrous insect' (Malcolm Pasley) or 'a giant bug' (J. A. Underwood). Stanley Corngold perhaps comes closest to the original with his 'monstrous vermin'. The proper names of Kafka's characters sometimes carry particular associations which are impossible to render in English and would require lengthy footnotes to explain. But perhaps the greatest difficulty for translators into English is Kafka's frequent use of the subjunctive. As I have discussed in relation to the opening of *The Trial*, this gives his narratives their characteristically ambivalent quality, infusing them with doubt and uncertainty, but is almost impossible to reproduce in a language which lacks the subjunctive mode.

Kafka scholarship: the challenge of interpretation

Kafka's texts have attracted a vast number of diverse and often conflicting responses, a situation which is itself something of a refrain in Kafka studies. With its shifting theoretical paradigms, Kafka scholarship reflects the more general developments within literary criticism over the last century. In this, Kafka is, of course, not alone. Writers and their texts have always been rediscovered by new generations of readers, and modernist texts, which are often experimental and multivalent, lend themselves particularly well to this undertaking. Kafka's works are part of the modernist canon, but they also have particular features that exacerbate this sense of openness.

More than most authors, Kafka embodies the challenge – or indeed the failure – of interpretation. The particular appeal of his texts lies in the way in which they both invite and resist explanation. Some texts seem simple at first sight and reveal their complexities only on closer inspection, while others are immediately puzzling and opaque. In any case, the more strongly we feel compelled to understand them, to resolve their internal contradictions, the more likely we are to fail. As we have seen in previous chapters, Kafka explicitly addresses this problem of interpretation. A prime example is the penultimate chapter of *The Trial*, where Josef K. and the priest discuss the legend about the man from the country. Whichever avenue K. pursues in trying to make sense of the story, the priest rejects it with reference to details in the text and to the readings of others. As this exchange in the *The Trial* shows, interpretation is an open-ended process, and every reader brings to the text his or her own preconceptions, which will jar both with the text and with the viewpoints of others. As the priest tells K., 'What is written is unchangeable, and opinions are often just an expression of despair at that' (*T* 157/*P* 198).

This statement could be the motto of Kafka criticism. Josef K. breaks off the conversation in despair, but it can be quite liberating to accept that Kafka's texts are intended to remain ambivalent, paradoxical and open-ended. One of its consequences is that any study, however thorough or elaborate, will come to only limited conclusions; in assessing any interpretation (including our own), we need to bear in mind the self-conscious challenge which Kafka's texts pose to interpretation. Thus we should judge any study by how closely it engages with the text – its motifs, style and structure, but also the mechanisms involved in the creation (and suspension) of meaning. Another, related question to ask is how effectively an interpretation resists the temptation to reduce the complexity of Kafka's texts to one overriding concern. A successful reading will take us closer to Kafka's texts and open up new perspectives, giving us the incentive to pursue our own enquiries.

Unfortunately, many Kafka studies fail on these counts. The consequences of ignoring the self-questioning nature of Kafka's texts are particularly apparent in early scholarship, where critics responded to the opacity of his writings by trying to 'decode' them, by extrapolating a (hidden) layer from the edifice of the text. Such readings are wedded to a medieval model of interpretation, whereby a text in its literal dimension is assumed to contain an encrypted 'allegorical' meaning. One of the main exponents of this allegorical approach was Max Brod, whose critical authority was strengthened by his role as Kafka's friend, editor and executor. As early as 1921, Brod started to develop his theological interpretations, emphasizing Kafka's status as a Jewish, Zionist writer. According to Brod, the institutions in Kafka's second and third novels, the court and the castle, represent the two manifestations of God in the Kabbalah, namely judgement and grace. In this generalizing approach, Brod was not alone. Other schools of thought, such as Existentialism and Marxism, used similar techniques, asserting that Kafka's texts expressed fear, nothingness and disgust, or Marxist class struggle and alienation.

Benjamin and Adorno: returning to the text

One of the earliest and most influential Kafka critics is the writer and thinker Walter Benjamin. In two pieces written in the 1930s, his radio essay 'Franz Kafka: *Beim Bau der chinesischen Mauer*' (1931) and the more extensive and influential 'Franz Kafka: On the Tenth Anniversary of his Death' (1934), he takes issue with allegorical interpretations. Conceding that Brod's claims – that *The Trial* depicts the divine judgement and *The Castle* divine grace – cannot actually be disproven, he concludes: 'The only problem is that such methods are far less productive than the admittedly much more challenging task of interpreting a writer from the center of his image world.'[1] Benjamin undertakes such a text-immanent interpretation in his essays, focusing on aspects such as the role of animals and other non-human creatures, on Kafka's various assistant figures, and on theatre and play-acting, the expressive yet opaque gestures of his characters, which complement and contradict the spoken dialogue.

Benjamin stays very close to Kafka's novels and short stories, most of which had only recently been published, and he quotes extensively from them, often letting the texts speak for themselves. Despite Benjamin's affiliations to

Marxism, he does not try to translate Kafka's works into a theoretical meta-discourse, but he does draw on other literary texts. Each of the four sections opens with an example taken from outside Kafka's work – an anecdote, story, nursery rhyme or parable, which Benjamin uses to highlight aspects of Kafka's work. The opening anecdote features Potemkin, the eighteenth-century Russian statesman, and is described by Benjamin as 'a herald of Kafka's work, storming two hundred years ahead of it',[2] while the second is not actually a text but a photograph of Kafka as a five-year-old boy, which Benjamin describes to shed light on Kafka's literary conception of childhood. Benjamin's aim, then, is not explanation or (conclusive) interpretation but an indirect method of illumination through analogy. He does not present Kafka's texts as the work of a solitary genius, but rather as part of a much wider tradition, which includes Jewish and Christian religious thought as well as anecdote and folklore. However, Benjamin's concern is not just with narrative figures and motifs, but also with underlying, cognitive processes which shape Kafka's texts: the dialectic of attentiveness and distraction, and of memory and forgetting, embodied in disfigured creatures such as Odradek.

The philosopher Theodor W. Adorno was a close friend of Benjamin's; his 'Notes on Kafka' (1953) build on Benjamin's ideas but are more openly political, inspired by the Marxist tenets of 'critical theory'. Adorno echoes many of Benjamin's points. Thus he argues that the trajectory of Kafka's texts leads away from the human into the world of the animal or the inanimate object, and he draws attention to the way in which the flow of his narratives is arrested by quasi-photographic tableaux, which are hyper-vivid and yet opaque. Although Adorno was no friend of the cinema, he uses film to illustrate what he calls the tactile intensity of Kafka's texts, arguing that they charge towards the reader 'like a locomotive in a three-dimensional film'.[3]

Adorno continues the anti-allegorical thrust of Benjamin's approach by stressing that Kafka's texts have to be taken literally at any cost: 'Each sentence is literal and each signifies ... Each sentence says "interpret me", and none will permit it.'[4] On the whole, though, Adorno's vision of Kafka is more negative than Benjamin's, and his reading contains the resonances of the recent catastrophe of the Holocaust. In an argument that anticipates his later *Aesthetic Theory* (published posthumously in 1970), Adorno argues that insight and critique in Kafka's text can no longer be articulated positively but only in the negative. For him, Kafka's texts uncover a universal truth about human existence – the individual's alienation in the modern, reified world – but they do so without pointing out alternatives: 'The subject seeks to break the spell of reification by reifying itself.'[5] By singling out alienation as the core concern of Kafka's texts, Adorno produces a persuasive and coherent reading, and yet he arguably falls into the trap of totalizing interpretation which he himself criticizes – the trap of trying to reduce Kafka's texts to one overarching message.

Benjamin's and Adorno's essays lay the foundations for future generations of Kafka scholars; resonances of their arguments and their method of close reading can be found in anti-hermeneutic, post-structuralist studies, as well as in philological and cultural-historical interpretations.

Psychoanalysis: Oedipus and beyond

One of the ways to fundamentally miss the point of Kafka's writings, Benjamin claimed, was via psychoanalytic criticism, and yet both he and Adorno acknowledged the many resonances of Freud's work in Kafka's writings. Stressing the role of parapraxis, dreams and neurosis in Kafka's texts, Adorno concludes: 'As though conducting an experiment, he studies what would happen if the results of psychoanalysis were to prove true not merely metaphorically but in the flesh.'[6] Psychoanalysis remains one of the most enduring strands of Kafka scholarship, and while its paradigms can sometimes appear rather repetitive and predictable, psychoanalytic criticism is not just concerned with textual motifs and their underlying ('latent') meaning, but with the overall structure of the narrative, the mechanisms – such as distortion, displacement and condensation – through which textual meaning is created and yet suspended.

An important contribution to psychoanalytic criticism, as well as a critique of Freudian frameworks, is Gilles Deleuze and Félix Guattari's *Kafka: Toward a Minor Literature* (1975). This slim book is indebted to Benjamin both methodologically, by working closely with Kafka's texts, and thematically. One of its main concerns is the close connection between power and desire. In a polemical rejection of Freud's Oedipus complex and the underlying incest taboo, the authors argue that patriarchal power does not restrict or repress desire but is a productive, proliferating force. As they write about *The Trial*, 'where one believed there was a law, there is in fact desire, and desire alone'.[7] Desire in Kafka's texts becomes 'deterritorialized', a linking device which operates not vertically, hierarchically, but horizontally, through a '*contiguity of desire* that causes whatever happens to happen in the office next door'.[8] Just as desire is contagious, ubiquitous, power in Kafka's texts is not a matter of vertical hierarchies, of a binary opposition between rulers and oppressed, but an immanent force field which encompasses all characters.

Such non-hierarchical structures also shape the architecture of Kafka's texts. In their introduction, the authors liken his writings to the burrow in Kafka's late fragment of the same title. Like the burrow, Kafka's texts have many entrances and exits, which are designed to trick the enemy – the critic trying to conquer, arrest their meaning. Here and elsewhere in their writings, Deleuze and Guattari use the term 'rhizome', which refers to a vertical, root-like structure where all parts carry the same weight and where each element is connected to all the others. There is, then, no privileged route into Kafka's texts, for 'none matters more than another'.[9]

Deleuze and Guattari's reading of Kafka is idiosyncratic and provocative, challenging critical orthodoxies. Theirs is a very different Kafka – not the exponent of existential angst and alienation, but an author whose texts playfully subvert modern power structures. One charge which can be levelled against their rhizomatic method is its arbitrariness; if all routes into the text are equally (in)valid, how can we differentiate between them? But Deleuze and Guattari's rather playful approach also has more serious implications. Expanding on Kafka's own reflections on 'minor literature', they emphasize the political dimension of his texts, their ability to speak on behalf of a collective, and yet by emphasizing the multi-valence of his texts, they defend the autonomy of literary discourse, whose complexity cannot be instrumentalized for a particular purpose.

Deconstruction

Deleuze and Guattari's study has had a major impact on post-structuralist approaches to Kafka, which were particularly prominent in the 1980s and 90s. Deconstruction is one of the chief strands of post-structuralism. It is less a self-contained theoretical discourse with its own set of claims or assumptions than a critical method that attempts to read texts against the grain, challenging the assumptions of traditional philology. The term 'deconstruction' was coined by its founder, the French philosopher Jacques Derrida. One of its key concepts is 'différance', which means both difference and deferral. Textual meaning is never 'present' in a text, for words and signs are only meaningful in relation to each other, and cannot summon, or capture, an extra-textual meaning.

For Derrida, Kafka's texts exemplify the precepts of deconstruction. In his 1982 lecture 'Before the Law', he explores Kafka's short story of the same title. As he argues, Kafka's text does not depict the Law, but *is* itself the Law, a fact which explains its hermetic, self-referential quality: 'The text guards itself, maintains itself – like the law, speaking only of itself, that is to say, of its non-identity with itself ... It is the law, makes the law and leaves the reader before the law.'[10] The Law, then, is the reference point behind all meaning, and yet it can be neither accessed nor represented. One of the cornerstones of hermeneutic criticism is the 'hermeneutic circle', the notion that our understanding of a text steadily increases with each reading, as we keep adding new insights to our overall picture. In Kafka's case, Derrida argues, re-reading does not lead to more comprehensive understanding; each reading is different from (and incompatible with) the next.

As the example of 'Before the Law' shows, Kafka's texts lend themselves particularly well to deconstructive readings. Kafka is, in a sense, a deconstructivist *avant la lettre* but, as a result, the deconstructive method is arguably of limited use, for it is at risk of merely repeating – in more elaborate but often rather repetitive terms – what is already present in the texts. Deconstruction does, however, have the advantage over other approaches that it engages with the inner working of Kafka's texts and brings out their self-reflexive, self-questioning character.

Cultural-historical readings

While deconstruction operates on the premise that literary texts are self-reflexive and ultimately non-representational, Kafka criticism since the 1980s has seen a return to a more historically grounded form of literary criticism. Literature is here considered in relation to other social practices and systems of representation; the aim is to contextualize Kafka's texts in new ways, bringing out resonances and influences. This is a wide and evolving field of enquiry; here I will just single out a few examples.

One strand of criticism has revisited Kafka's relationship to philosophy and religion, particularly Judaism – not through the allegorical, speculative methods of early criticism but through a thorough examination of sources, texts and contexts that might have shaped Kafka's writings down to details of motifs and storylines. A second group of studies has traced Kafka's relation to his literary context, including his reception of the work of literary predecessors (such as Goethe, Kleist, Flaubert and Dostoevsky) and contemporaries. A third group, finally, has focused on Kafka's relationship to contemporary culture, including both high art movements, such as Expressionism and the fin de siècle, and mass entertainment, with particular reference to technical media such as the gramophone, film and photography. Whatever the focus of these studies, however, one point applies across the field of cultural-historical Kafka criticism. The best research demonstrates not just how the historical context is reflected in Kafka's texts on an explicit, thematic level, but how other cultural discourses and paradigms affect the inner workings of his texts, their poetological, self-reflexive dimension.

Kafka in film: the challenge of adaptation

There is probably no art form or medium on which Kafka's texts have not left their traces. He has inspired visual artists and filmmakers, composers, playwrights and novelists from around the world, and his influence crosses the boundary between high and popular culture. Thus his texts have had a particularly strong influence on graphic artists, and Kafka is omnipresent on the Internet, where a search brings up countless websites dedicated to his life and works, to his drawings and photographs, and to Kafka research, as well as more quirky and imaginative sites such as blogs and adventure games.

Kafka's huge influence on the arts is the result of two factors. His texts are odd and disturbing, and their simple but memorable storylines lend themselves well to be adapted and developed. Irrespective of their strangeness, however, his texts portray moods and experiences that are universally recognizable. At heart, they are concerned with the pitfalls of modern life in ways which still seem fresh and relevant today. Kafka is a truly global author, and although his texts are rooted in their time and context, they do not – at least at first reading – require in-depth historical knowledge but continue to resonate with people from all walks of life. This, arguably, is both a strength and a weakness. Since the term 'Kafkaesque' was coined in 1936 by the British poet Cecil Day Lewis, it has become a neat shorthand for all manner of alien or unsettling situations, but the ubiquity of the term is also symptomatic of a problem, suggesting that we are somehow familiar with Kafka's works even if we have never read a word of them.

Although the challenges faced by artists responding to Kafka are very different from those of Kafka scholars, there are many points of contact between the two. Kafka's reception in different art forms has become an important part of Kafka research, while artists' responses are often informed by critical debates. Both forms of response revolve around similar questions, most importantly the problem of interpretation, which in the creative arts feeds into the challenge of adapting or 'translating' Kafka into a different medium. To illustrate these cross-connections, I will now turn to three landmark films based on Kafka's novels, which give an insight into different methods of adaptation across four decades.

Orson Welles, *The Trial*

Orson Welles's *The Trial* (France, Italy, Germany 1962) is a modern classic and the most famous of all Kafka film adaptations. Welles stated in an interview that he regarded *The Trial* as his best film, although audience responses were mixed. Kafka purists disliked the liberties Welles took with the novel, and film critics, looking for a second *Citizen Kane*, were disappointed by its abstract quality. *The Trial* is the earliest of the three adaptations discussed here, and the one where the director exerts his creative authority most freely, although by amending the storyline in the way he did, Welles was arguably trying to bring out the essence of Kafka's novel. Welles turns *The Trial* into a McCarthyist thriller about surveillance and (political) persecution. The theme of sexual guilt looms large at the beginning; Fräulein Bürstner's name is mentioned in the very first sentence, and K. asserts unprompted that the policemen will not find any pornographic material in his room. Subsequently, however, K. hints that his arrest might have a political cause, a revelation that triggers a shocked response in his conversation with Fräulein Bürstner.

Welles wrote the screenplay and also played the advocate, Albert Hastler, a character based on the novel's advocate, Huld. In the film, his role is expanded, for after K. has dismissed him, he makes another appearance just before the end, after K.'s meeting with the priest. Anthony Perkins is a handsome, sinewy Josef K. and bears a striking resemblance to Kafka as we know him from photographs (see Fig. 6 on p. 106). He invests his part with a sense of black comedy, though in the course of the film his initial hysterical surprise gradually gives way to more aggressive behaviour.

The setting of Welles's film is more sleekly modern and yet more dilapidated than Kafka's novel. Josef K.'s workplace at the bank is in a vast open-plan office filled with the deafening noise of hundreds of typists, and Welles also adds a scene in which K. takes his uncle to see the bank's central computer, which, as the uncle suggests, might have the answer to his case. The scenes set at the law offices were filmed in the (then disused) Gare d'Orsay in Paris, a space both vast and labyrinthine. Other parts of the film were filmed in Zagreb; the apartment block where K. lives is a Soviet-style housing estate surrounded by an urban waste dump, evoking inhuman living conditions at the height of the Cold War.

The film alludes to the political witch hunt of the McCarthy era, as well as the more general anonymity of modern life, but it also contains a brief, cryptic scene which has more specific resonances. On his way to his first hearing, K. passes a large group of dishevelled-looking elderly men and women, who are waiting outside, wrapped in sheets, with numbered signs around their necks – a sight which recalls the deportations of the Third Reich. The revised ending, in turn, marks an attempt to update Kafka's novel and imbue it with contemporary relevance. Rather than slaying K. with a butcher's knife, his executioners throw him a bomb, which K. picks up before it explodes in a mushroom cloud – *The Trial* for the nuclear age.

Perhaps the most memorable change that Welles makes to the structure of the novel, however, concerns the priest's legend, which in his film appears not close to the end but at the beginning, as a kind of prologue. The story about the man from country, which is read by Welles himself, is accompanied by a series of atmospheric black-and-white tableaux, pinscreen scenes by the artist Alexandre Alexeïeff. They highlight the timeless, static quality of the legend and give it the function of a narrative frontispiece. Leading over from the legend to the film, Welles declares that it has the 'logic of a dream, a nightmare', thus preparing the viewer for the dreamlike events which are to follow. The last of these stills recurs at the very end of the film, accompanied by the director's voice: 'My name is Orson Welles' – a verbal signature with which Welles asserts his own creative authority over Kafka's text.

Straub/Huillet, *Class Relations*

The film *Class Relations* (*Klassenverhältnisse*, Germany, France 1984) by the French husband-and-wife team Jean-Marie Straub and Danièle Huillet is an adaptation of Kafka's first novel, *The Man who Disappeared*. Their title spells out the element of social criticism implicit in Kafka's novel. Shot in black and white, it uses a Brechtian technique of defamiliarization, which is particularly noticeable in the acting style, but also in the disjuncture between soundtrack and camerawork, and in the directors' more general principle of adaptation. Their aim, as they declare in an interview, is to dissect the text, to strip it down to its skeleton, its spine, and thereby to open it up to scrutiny.[11]

The actors act and talk in a strangely contrived way. The lead actor, Christian Heinisch, 'plays the role of Karl as if he is a showroom dummy'.[12] His pauses in mid-sentence transform his speech into a kind of stilted verse; the small pauses give the viewer just enough time to try to anticipate the next word, but this expectation is often defied, underlining the ambiguity of Kafka's text. Many but not all characters speak in this manner, as speech patterns are used to mark out differences in social status. Karl, the most downtrodden of all, speaks most haltingly, while his wealthy uncle, played by Mario Adorf, comes across as lively and naturalistic.

The camerawork is central to the film's political message. To enforce the viewer's Brechtian detachment, scenes are often shot from mid-distance, and the camerawork is very static. We rarely get close-ups of characters' faces; the effect of this is particularly disorienting when a new character is introduced but we do not get a good view of them until much later (if at all). In other scenes, though, the camera lingers in an intrusive, unnerving way. When Karl meets the stoker, we get a long, static shot of him listening, with his eyes closed, to the entire American national anthem played by a remote brass band. Another static shot shows Karl reading his uncle's farewell letter, although this letter's content, a turning point in the novel, is never communicated to the viewer.

As viewers, we are either too close to the action or not close enough, but never at the 'right' distance. This sense of disorientation is enforced by the repeated disjuncture between sound and image. In dialogues between two characters, the camera does not switch between the two but remains focused on the more passive character while the voice of the speaker off-screen is recessed, forcing us to concentrate hard on what they are saying.

In an interview, the directors declared that their aim had been to do 'the opposite of what Orson Welles did; we didn't want to show in any way what Kafka described'.[13] This is borne out in their screenplay; in adapting Kafka's novel, they leave out all the 'cinematically' animated scenes which in the text convey the disorienting dynamism of American life. Thus the film misses out the brief 'cuts' to the moving ships in the harbour, which in the novel are interspersed with the discussion in the captain's office, as well as the panorama of the bustling streets of New York City, in which Karl gets absorbed when standing on the balcony in his uncle's house. In the film, this latter scene is replaced by a long tracking shot of tall town houses filmed from below, suggesting Karl's dwarfed perspective. The scenes set in New York City were shot in Hamburg, a reflection of the fact that Kafka himself had never travelled to the United States and that his protagonist is weighed down by his (literal and metaphorical) European baggage.

At this early point, the camerawork suggests, Karl's journey is still wide open, but in the second half of the film the scenes are shot mostly in claustrophobic interiors. In the part set at the Hotel Occidental, the bustle of the large hotel, which is such a prominent theme in Kafka's novel, is completely missing. Instead, we get many close-ups of Karl standing alone next to his elevator, and when he carries the drunken Robinson to his bed, he takes him to a small, quiet room rather than the crowded liftboys' dormitory. The film is beautifully shot, but sparse and empty. By focusing on the impassive protagonist, a character drained of all emotion, it depicts not the unceasing traffic of American life but its underlying solitude.

This is underlined by another aspect of the camerawork. The camera often lingers on empty rooms or spaces after characters have left. Spaces and objects gain an eerie life of their own, which is inaccessible to the people living among them. Indeed, the long, lingering shots of empty spaces, which also include desolate landscapes and motorways, suggest a world devoid of human beings; in this, they encapsulate the notion of 'disappearance' in the novel's title and anticipate what is not actually depicted in the text: the protagonist's death. As the directors remark, 'What Kafka has written could only have come from a young man, but to really sense or discover what Kafka is all about you have to be close to the grave.'[14]

Class Relations is radically, provocatively different from mainstream cinema. Watching the film is not an enjoyable experience but requires considerable endurance. Straub/Huillet are not inspired by philological reverence for the original; they adapt and alter the novel in ways that make it more appropriate to the cinematic medium and bring out its unique qualities, not as a medium of illusionist immersion, but as a visual object – strange but strangely beautiful – which challenges our viewing habits and expectations.

Michael Haneke, *The Castle*

The Austrian director Michael Haneke is known for his stark, disturbing films, such as *Benny's Video* (1992), *Funny Games* (1997) and *Caché* (2005). *The Castle* (*Das Schloss*, Austria 1997), which was produced for television, is a much more low-key affair and lacks the graphic violence which characterizes much of his work. Haneke's *The Castle* is the most textually faithful of the three adaptations discussed here, though it has been criticized as rather 'tame' and unimaginative. That said, Haneke does subtly add his own emphasis, and his use of sound and camerawork is reminiscent of Straub/Huillet's Brechtian adaptation.

To emphasize the film's proximity to the novel, an off-screen narrator (Udo Samel) reads out excerpts from the text, which provide a commentary on the unfolding events. As in *Class Relations*, the visual and auditory channels are often separated. Thus Olga's dance with the coarse servants, which is described in detail by the off-screen narrator, is barely visible in the background, and in dialogues the camerawork is disorientatingly asymmetrical. In some scenes, the person K. is talking to can only be heard from the off, and even where two characters are shown in conversation, the camera lingers on one of them rather than following the rhythm of the dialogue.

Haneke's adaptation closely follows the plotline of the novel, but he places his own emphasis through shortening and omission. Olga's account of how her family came to be ostracized from the village community, which in the novel takes up about fifty pages, is summarized in a few sentences, and K.'s conversations with the landlady Gardena, and with the secretaries Momus and Bürgel are also shortened. The actor Ulrich Mühe effectively conveys K.'s mixture of vulnerability, cunning and aggression. Overall, though, the storyline of his struggle against the castle authorities is toned down to make more room for his personal relations, most notably the relationship between K. and Frieda (Susanne Lothar), which is traced in close, psychological detail.

There are, however, some instances where Haneke departs from the novel in more obvious ways. The film contains no shots of the castle, which in the novel is clearly visible above the village, and likewise there are no shots of Klamm when K. observes him through the peephole. The film thus edits out all visual evidence of the castle's and Klamm's physical existence, transforming them into figments of K.'s, and the viewer's, imagination.

Another intervention are the thirty fade-outs into black which are inserted into the film, lasting about three seconds each. They are used to separate scenes from each other, but are sometimes placed in the middle of a scene, thus highlighting the inherent fragmentation of a novel that was written as one continuous text. This emphasis on the novel as fragment is most apparent at the very end. The soundtrack of the film ends abruptly, with the narrator reading out the final, unfinished sentence of the manuscript. Interestingly, though, here image and soundtrack once again diverge. The passage read out by the narrator describes K.'s arrival at Gerstäcker's cottage, where he is about to have a conversation with Gerstäcker's old mother. The final shot, however, lags behind the storyline, for it shows K. and Gerstäcker on their way to the cottage, but fades out before their arrival. The abrupt finality of Kafka's novel is thus counterbalanced by the film's open-ended journey, its potential to reach beyond the confines of the text.

The three film versions discussed here, then, are as diverse as the methods of Kafka criticism. Kafka's enduring fascination for readers of all backgrounds is rooted in his resistance to interpretation, translation and adaptation, a resistance which continues to spark fruitful, ongoing engagement and debate.

Notes

1 Life

1. Peter-André Alt, *Franz Kafka: Der ewige Sohn* (Munich: Beck, 2005); Reiner Stach, *Kafka: The Decisive Years*, trans. Shelley Frisch (San Diego, CA: Harcourt, 2005). The second volume of Stach's three-part biography, *Kafka: Die Jahre der Erkenntnis* (Frankfurt/Main: Fischer, 2008), will appear in English with Princeton University Press in 2013. Alt's biography is due to appear in English with Northwestern University Press.
2. Stach, *Jahre der Erkenntnis*, 90.

2 Contexts

1. Georg Simmel, 'The Metropolis and Mental Life', in *The Blackwell City Reader*, ed. Gary Bridge and Sophie Watson, 2nd edn (Oxford: Wiley-Blackwell, 2010), 103–10 (103–4).
2. Max Weber, *The Protestant Ethic and the 'Spirit' of Capitalism and Other Writings*, ed., trans. and intro. Peter Baehr and Gordon C. Welles (London: Penguin, 2002), 121.
3. Sigmund Freud, *The Standard Edition of the Complete Psychological Works of Sigmund Freud*, trans. and ed. James Strachey, 24 vols. (London: Hogarth Press, 1973), II, 160.
4. Freud, *Standard Edition*, XXII, 80.
5. Gilles Deleuze and Félix Guattari, *Kafka: Toward a Minor Literature*, trans. Dana Polan (Minneapolis: University of Minnesota Press, 1986), 17.

3 Works

1. Alfred Polgar, 'The Small Form', in *The Vienna Coffeehouse Wits, 1890–1938*, trans., ed. and intro. Harold B. Segel (West Lafayette, IN: Purdue University Press, 1993), 279–81 (280).
2. Walter Benjamin, 'Drei Bücher', in *Gesammelte Schriften*, ed. Rolf Tiedemann and Hermann Schweppenhäuser, 7 vols., paperback edn (Frankfurt/Main: Suhrkamp, 1991), III, 107–13 (110).

3. On the centrality of the concept for Kafka's works, see Mark Anderson, *Kafka's Clothes: Ornament and Aestheticism in the Habsburg Fin de Siècle* (Oxford: Oxford University Press, 1992), 22–3 and passim.

4. Gilles Deleuze and Félix Guattari, *Kafka: Toward a Minor Literature*, trans. Dana Polan (Minneapolis: University of Minnesota Press, 1986), 14–15.

5. Benjamin, 'Franz Kafka: On the Tenth Anniversary of his Death', in *Selected Writings*, ed. Michael W. Jennings, 4 vols. (Cambridge, MA: Belknap Press, 1996–2003), II, 794–818 (800).

6. Max Horkheimer, 'The End of Reason', in *The Essential Frankfurt School Reader*, ed. Andrew Arato and Eike Gebhardt (New York: Continuum, 1982), 26–48 (37–8).

7. See Ritchie Robertson, *Kafka: Judaism, Politics, and Literature* (Oxford: Clarendon Press, 1985), 90–3.

8. Walter Benjamin, *The Arcades Project*, ed. Rolf Tiedemann, trans. Howard Eiland and Kevin McLaughlin (Cambridge, MA: Harvard University Press, 1999) 389; 391.

9. Benjamin, 'Franz Kafka: On the Tenth Anniversary of his Death', II, 794–818 (802).

10. Kurt Tucholsky, 'In der Strafkolonie', *Die Weltbühne*, 3 June 1920.

11. Benjamin, 'Franz Kafka: On the Tenth Anniversary of his Death', II, 497–8.

12. Roland Barthes, 'The Death of the Author', in *Image-Music-Text*, trans. Stephen Heath (New York: Hill & Wang, 1977), 142–8 (148).

13. Sigmund Freud, *The Standard Edition of the Complete Psychological Works of Sigmund Freud*, trans. and ed. James Strachey, 24 vols. (London: Hogarth Press, 1973), XVI, 284–5.

14. Elizabeth Boa and Rachel Palfreyman, *Heimat. A German Dream: Regional Loyalties and National Identity in German Culture, 1890–1990* (Oxford: Oxford University Press, 2000), 1.

15. W. G. Sebald, 'The Undiscover'd Country: The Death Motif in Kafka's *Castle*', *Journal of European Studies*, 2 (1972), 22–34 (34).

16. Robertson, *Kafka: Judaism*, 358–61.

17. Elizabeth Boa, *Kafka: Gender, Class, and Race in the Letters and Fictions* (Oxford: Clarendon Press, 1996), 178.

4 Scholarship and adaptations

1. Walter Benjamin, 'Franz Kafka: *Beim Bau der chinesischen Mauer*', in *Selected Writings*, ed. Michael W. Jennings, 4 vols. (Cambridge, MA: Belknap Press, 1996–2003), II, 494–500 (495).

2. Walter Benjamin, 'Franz Kafka: On the Tenth Anniversary of his Death', in *Selected Writings*, ed. Jennings, II, 794–818 (795).

3. Theodor W. Adorno, 'Notes on Kafka', in *Prisms*, trans. Shierry Weber and Samuel Weber (Cambridge, MA: MIT Press, 1983), 243–71 (246).

4. Adorno, 'Notes on Kafka', 246.

5. Adorno, 'Notes on Kafka', 270.

6. Adorno, 'Notes on Kafka', 251.
7. Gilles Deleuze and Félix Guattari, *Kafka: Toward a Minor Literature*, trans. Dana Polan (Minneapolis: University of Minnesota Press, 1986), 49.
8. Deleuze and Guattari, *Kafka*, 50.
9. Deleuze and Guattari, *Kafka*, 3.
10. Jacques Derrida, 'Before the Law', in *Acts of Literature*, ed. Derek Attridge (London: Routledge, 1992), 181–220 (211).
11. Cited in Martin Brady and Helen Hughes, 'Kafka Adapted to Film', in *The Cambridge Companion to Franz Kafka*, ed. Julian Preece (Cambridge: Cambridge University Press, 2002), 226–41 (234).
12. Marino Guida, 'Resisting Performance: Straub/Huillet's Filming of Kafka's *Der Verschollene*', in *Performance and Performativity in German Cultural Studies*, ed. Carolin Duttlinger, Lucia Ruprecht and Andrew Webber (Oxford: Lang, 2003), 121–35 (122).
13. Guida, 'Resisting Performance', 121.
14. Cited in Guida, 'Resisting Performance', 123–4.

Guide to further reading

Editions of Kafka's works

English

The Blue Octavo Notebooks, ed. Max Brod, trans. Ernst Kaiser and Eithne Wilkins
(Cambridge, MA: Exact Change, 1991)
The Castle, trans. Anthea Bell (Oxford: Oxford University Press, 2009)
The Complete Stories, ed. Nahum N. Glatzer (New York: Schocken, 1976)
The Diaries of Franz Kafka, 1910–23, ed. Max Brod (London: Minerva, 1992)
A Hunger Artist and Other Stories, trans. Joyce Crick (Oxford: Oxford University
Press, 2012)
Letters to Felice, ed. Erich Heller and Jürgen Born, trans. James Stern and Elisabeth
Duckworth (London: Minerva, 1992)
Letters to Friends, Family and Editors, trans. Richard Winston and Clara Winston
(Richmond: Oneworld Classics, 2011)
Letters to Milena, ed. Willy Haas, trans. Tania and James Stern (London:
Minerva, 1992)
The Man who Disappeared (America), trans. Ritchie Robertson (Oxford: Oxford
University Press, 2012)
The Metamorphosis and Other Stories, trans. Joyce Crick (Oxford: Oxford
University Press, 2009)
The Office Writings, ed. Stanley Corngold, Jack Greenberg and Benno Wagner,
trans. Eric Patton with Ruth Hein (Princeton: Princeton University
Press, 2008)
The Trial, trans. Mike Mitchell (Oxford: Oxford University Press, 2009)

German

Amtliche Schriften, ed. Klaus Hermsdorf and Benno Wagner. Franz Kafka:
Schriften, Tagebücher, Briefe: Kritische Ausgabe (Frankfurt/Main:
Fischer, 2004)
Briefe 1900–1912, ed. Hans-Gerd Koch. Franz Kafka: Schriften, Tagebücher,
Briefe: Kritische Ausgabe (Frankfurt/Main: Fischer, 1999)

Briefe 1913–März 1914, ed. Hans-Gerd Koch. Franz Kafka: Schriften, Tagebücher, Briefe: Kritische Ausgabe (Frankfurt/Main: Fischer, 2001)

Briefe April 1914–1917, ed. Hans-Gerd Koch. Franz Kafka: Schriften, Tagebücher, Briefe: Kritische Ausgabe (Frankfurt/Main: Fischer, 2005)

Briefe 1902–1924, ed. Max Brod (Frankfurt/Main: Fischer, 1975)

Briefe an die Eltern aus den Jahren 1922–1924, ed. Josef Čermák and Martin Svatoš (Frankfurt/Main: Fischer, 1993)

Briefe an Felice und andere Korrespondenz aus der Verlobungszeit, ed. Erich Heller and Jürgen Born (Frankfurt/Main: Fischer, 1998)

Briefe an Milena, ed. Jürgen Born and Michael Müller, extended and revised edn (Frankfurt/Main: Fischer, 1999)

Drucke zu Lebzeiten, ed. Wolf Kittler, Hans-Gerd Koch and Gerhard Neumann. Franz Kafka: Schriften, Tagebücher, Briefe: Kritische Ausgabe (Frankfurt/Main: Fischer, 1996)

Drucke zu Lebzeiten: Apparatband, ed. Wolf Kittler, Hans-Gerd Koch and Gerhard Neumann. Franz Kafka: Schriften, Tagebücher, Briefe: Kritische Ausgabe (Frankfurt/Main: Fischer, 1996)

Nachgelassene Schriften und Fragmente I, ed. Malcolm Pasley. Franz Kafka: Schriften, Tagebücher, Briefe: Kritische Ausgabe (Frankfurt/Main: Fischer, 1993)

Nachgelassene Schriften und Fragmente II, ed. Jost Schillemeit. Franz Kafka: Schriften, Tagebücher, Briefe: Kritische Ausgabe (Frankfurt/Main: Fischer, 1992)

Der Proceß, ed. Malcolm Pasley. Franz Kafka: Schriften, Tagebücher, Briefe: Kritische Ausgabe (Frankfurt/Main: Fischer, 1990)

Der Proceß: Apparatband, ed. Malcolm Pasley. Franz Kafka: Schriften, Tagebücher, Briefe: Kritische Ausgabe (Frankfurt/Main: Fischer, 1990)

Das Schloß, ed. Malcolm Pasley. Franz Kafka: Schriften, Tagebücher, Briefe: Kritische Ausgabe (Frankfurt/Main: Fischer, 1982)

Das Schloß: Apparatband, ed. Malcolm Pasley. Franz Kafka: Schriften, Tagebücher, Briefe: Kritische Ausgabe (Frankfurt/Main: Fischer, 1982)

Tagebücher, ed. Hans-Gerd Koch, Michael Müller and Malcolm Pasley. Franz Kafka: Schriften, Tagebücher, Briefe: Kritische Ausgabe (Frankfurt/Main: Fischer, 1990)

Der Verschollene, ed. Jost Schillemeit. Franz Kafka: Schriften, Tagebücher, Briefe: Kritische Ausgabe (Frankfurt/Main: Fischer, 1983)

Other primary sources

Adorno, Theodor W., *Prisms*, trans. Shierry Weber and Samuel Weber (Cambridge, MA: MIT Press, 1983)

Benjamin, Walter, *The Arcades Project*, ed. Rolf Tiedemann, trans. Howard Eiland and Kevin McLaughlin (Cambridge, MA: Harvard University Press, 1999)

Selected Writings, ed. Michael W. Jennings, 4 vols. (Cambridge, MA: Belknap Press of Harvard University Press, 1996–2003)
Freud, Sigmund, *The Standard Edition of the Complete Psychological Works of Sigmund Freud*, trans. and ed. James Strachey, 24 vols. (London: Hogarth Press, 1973)

Select bibliography of secondary literature

Biography

Adler, Jeremy, *Franz Kafka* (London: Penguin, 2001). A concise and richly illustrated biography.
Brod, Max, *Franz Kafka: A Biography*, trans. G. Humphreys Roberts and Richard Winston (New York: Schocken, 1960). A biased but illuminating account of Kafka's life by his close friend.
Gilman, Sander L., *Franz Kafka* (London: Reaktion Books, 2005). Explores the relationship between Kafka's life and his work, focusing in particular on his Jewish identity and his relationship to his own body.
Hayman, Ronald, *K: A Biography of Kafka* (London: Weidenfeld & Nicolson, 1981). A clear, detailed account by a professional biographer who is at home with German.
Northey, Anthony, *Kafka's Relatives: Their Lives and His Writing* (New Haven: Yale University Press, 1991). This richly illustrated book traces the life stories of Kafka's wider family and their often exotic careers and experiences, which have left traces in Kafka's writings.
Stach, Reiner, *Kafka: The Decisive Years*, trans. Shelley Frisch (San Diego: Harcourt, 2005). Stach's well-researched and engaging account of the 'middle period' of Kafka's life, 1910–15, forms part of a three-part biography. The volume covering the years 1916–24 will appear in English with Princeton University Press in 2013, and the author is currently working on the volume on Kafka's childhood and youth.
Wagenbach, Klaus, *Kafka*, trans. Ewald Osers (Cambridge, MA: Harvard University Press, 2003). A concise account of Kafka's life by this veteran Kafka critic and biographer.

Historical context

Anderson, Mark M., *Reading Kafka: Prague, Politics, and the Fin de Siècle* (New York: Schocken, 1989). A collection of essays on Kafka's cultural context, which includes translated extracts from the work of important German critics such as Gerhard Neumann, Reiner Stach and Klaus Wagenbach.
Kieval, Hillel J., *The Making of Czech Jewry: National Conflict and Jewish Society in Bohemia, 1870–1918* (New York: Oxford University Press, 1988). Focuses

on the Czech-Jewish movement and Prague Zionism as the two dominant responses by Bohemian Jews to their changing environment.

Spector, Scott, *Prague Territories: National Conflict and Cultural Innovation in Franz Kafka's Fin de Siècle* (Berkeley: University of California Press, 2000). Explores the ethnic, linguistic and political conditions which shaped the work of Kafka and other German-speaking Jewish intellectuals in early-twentieth-century Prague.

Critical studies

Anderson, Mark M., *Kafka's Clothes: Ornament and Aestheticism in the Habsburg Fin de Siècle* (Oxford: Clarendon Press, 1992). Wide-ranging and original readings, which place Kafka in the context of contemporary literary discourses and cultural practices.

Beck, Evelyn Torton, *Kafka and the Yiddish Theatre: Its Impact on his Work* (Madison, WI: University of Wisconsin Press, 1971). Explores Kafka's passion for the Yiddish theatre and the traces this left in his writings.

Bernheimer, Charles, *Flaubert and Kafka: Studies in Psychopoetic Structure* (New Haven: Yale University Press, 1982). A psychoanalytically informed study, which stresses the analogies between the linguistic structures of Flaubert's and Kafka's texts and psychological processes such as condensation and displacement.

Boa, Elizabeth, *Kafka: Gender, Class, and Race in the Letters and Fictions* (Oxford: Clarendon Press, 1996). An engaging and readable study, which uncovers the complex network of ideas surrounding gender, class and race in Kafka's writings.

'Karl Rossmann, or the Boy who Wouldn't Grow Up: The Flight from Manhood in Kafka's *Der Verschollene*', in *From Goethe to Gide: Feminism, Aesthetics and the Literary Canon in France and Germany 1770–1930*, ed. Mary Orr and Lesley Sharpe (Exeter: University of Exeter Press, 2005), 168–83. A feminist reading of Kafka's first novel.

Bruce, Iris, *Kafka and Cultural Zionism: Dates in Palestine* (Madison, WI: University of Wisconsin Press, 2007). Explores Kafka's interest in Zionism and the presence of Jewish motifs in his literary works.

Canetti, Elias, *Kafka's Other Trial: The Letters to Felice*, trans. Christopher Middleton (London: Penguin Classics, 2012). Canetti's perceptive psychological study, first published in 1969, describes Kafka as 'the greatest expert on power'.

Corngold, Stanley, *Franz Kafka: The Necessity of Form* (Ithaca: Cornell University Press, 1988). Post-structuralist readings, which focus on the role of rhetorical tropes (such as metaphor and chiasmus) in Kafka's texts.

Lambent Traces: Franz Kafka (Princeton: Princeton University Press, 2004). Traces the implications of Kafka's literary breakthrough, with 'The Judgement', for his 'ecstatic' model of writing.

Corngold, Stanley (ed. and trans.), *Franz Kafka, The Metamorphosis: Translation, Backgrounds and Contexts, Criticism* (New York: Norton, 1996). Contains a translation of Kafka's novella as well as extracts from influential recent critical studies.

Corngold, Stanley and Benno Wagner, *Franz Kafka: The Ghosts in the Machine* (Chicago: Northwestern University Press, 2011). Taking Kafka's post at the Workers' Accident Insurance Company as their starting point, the authors argue that the conflict between individual and statistic is central to Kafka's work.

Deleuze, Gilles and Félix Guattari, *Kafka: Toward a Minor Literature*, trans. Dana Polan (Minneapolis: University of Minnesota Press, 1986). An influential study, which challenges classically Freudian, Oedipal interpretations, arguing that Kafka's texts facilitate a 'deterritorialization' of desire.

Derrida, Jacques, 'Before the Law', in *Acts of Literature*, ed. Derek Attridge (London: Routledge, 1992), 181–220. An influential example of a deconstructive approach to Kafka.

Dodd, William J., *Kafka: Der Proceß* (Glasgow: University of Glasgow French and German Publications, 1991). An introduction to Kafka's novel.

Kafka and Dostoevsky: The Shaping of Influence (London: Macmillan, 1992). Examines Dostoevsky's profound influence on Kafka in the years 1912–15.

Dodd, William J. (ed.), *Kafka: The Metamorphosis, The Trial and The Castle* (London: Longman, 1995). This volume assembles extracts of influential recent critical studies of these three Kafka texts alongside early responses and reviews.

Dowden, Stephen D., *Kafka's 'The Castle' and the Critical Imagination* (Columbia: Camden House, 1995). A survey of critical responses to Kafka's last novel which places them in their cultural and intellectual context, followed by the author's own interpretation.

Duttlinger, Carolin, *Kafka and Photography* (Oxford: Oxford University Press, 2007). Kafka was fascinated as well as unsettled by photography, and this study traces his recurring, life-long engagement with the medium in the fiction, diaries and letters.

'Franz Kafka, *Der Proceß*', in *Landmarks in the German Novel*, vol. I, ed. Peter Hutchinson (Oxford: Lang, 2007), 135–50. Focuses on the unfinished chapters of the novel and the ways they point beyond the (spatial, temporal and psychological) boundaries of Kafka's novel.

Engel, Manfred and Ritchie Robertson (eds.), *Kafka and Short Modernist Prose* (Würzburg: Königshausen & Neumann, 2010). The essays in this bilingual (English and German) volume explore Kafka's short prose works in the context of those produced by other modernist writers.

Gelber, Mark H. (ed.), *Kafka, Zionism and Beyond* (Tübingen: Niemeyer, 2004). This essay collection traces Kafka's attitude towards Zionism in relation to his life, work and connections with other writers.

Gilman, Sander L., *Franz Kafka: The Jewish Patient* (New York: Routledge, 1995). Gilman reconstructs the anti-Semitic discourse around 1900, arguing that it deeply affected Kafka, like many of his Jewish contemporaries, and is reflected in his sense of identity and in his works.

Marson, Eric L., *Kafka's Trial: The Case against Josef K.* (St Lucia, Queensland: University of Queensland Press, 1975). A detailed study, which draws out the connections between motifs and events in *The Trial* as well as its overarching concerns.

Pascal, Roy, *Kafka's Narrators: A Study of his Stories and Sketches* (Cambridge: Cambridge University Press, 1982). Traces the development of Kafka's narrative voice in the short prose works, from the mostly impersonal narrative perspective of the earlier pieces to his growing preference for personal narrators in the texts written after 1920.

Politzer, Heinz, *Franz Kafka: Parable and Paradox*, extended and revised edn (Ithaca: Cornell University Press, 1966). A classic, wide-ranging study, which argues that the paradoxical parable is one of the core forms of Kafka's prose.

Preece, Julian (ed.), *The Cambridge Companion to Kafka* (Cambridge: Cambridge University Press, 2002). Contains essays on Kafka's fictional and auto-biographical writings, on different ways of reading Kafka and on editions, translations and reception.

Robertson, Ritchie, *Kafka: Judaism, Politics, and Literature* (Oxford: Oxford University Press, 1985). A seminal investigation of the role of Judaism in Kafka's writings.

'Reading the Clues: Kafka, *Der Proceß*', in *The German Novel in the Twentieth Century: Beyond Realism*, ed. David Midgley (Edinburgh: Edinburgh University Press, 1993), 59–79. A good introduction to *The Trial*, which shows how it emerges from the realist literary tradition but subverts its precepts.

'In Search of the Historical Kafka: A Selective Review of Research, 1980–92', *The Modern Language Review*, 89 (1994), 107–37. A survey of studies that explore Kafka's texts in relation to their historical and cultural context.

Kafka: A Very Short Introduction (Oxford: Oxford University Press, 2004). A thematically organized, wide-ranging yet concise introduction to Kafka's life and works.

Rolleston, James, *A Companion to the Works of Franz Kafka* (Rochester, NY: Camden House, 2002). Contains essays on Kafka's principal prose texts, though not on the diaries and letters, as well as two articles on critical editions of his works. Compared to the *Cambridge Companion*, the angle of some of the essays is more deliberately specific.

Sheppard, Richard W., *On Kafka's Castle: A Study* (London: Croom Helm, 1973). Puts particular emphasis on the independent perspective offered by the novel's 'implicit narrator' and on Kafka's 'alienation devices'.

Sokel, Walter H., *The Myth of Power and the Self: Essays on Franz Kafka* (Detroit: Wayne State University Press, 2002). The assembled essays, by a

veteran Kafka critic, explore the relationship between power and the self
in Kafka's writings.

Speirs, Ronald and Beatrice Sandberg, *Franz Kafka.* Macmillan Modern Novelists
(Basingstoke: Macmillan, 1997). Accessible interpretations of Kafka's
three novels.

Triffitt, Gregory B., *Kafka's 'Landarzt' Collection: Rhetoric and Interpretation*
(New York: Lang, 1985). Focuses on the inner logic of the *Country Doctor*
collection and on correspondences between particular stories.

Webber, Andrew, 'Kafka, Die Verwandlung', in Peter Hutchinson (ed.),
Landmarks in German Short Prose (Oxford: Lang, 2003), 175–90.
A theoretical reading of the novella which relates it in particular to Julia
Kristeva's theory of abjection.

Zilcosky, John, *Kafka's Travels: Exoticism, Colonialism, and the Traffic of Writing*
(New York: Palgrave, 2003). Explores the theme of travel in Kafka's texts
in the light of contemporary discourses about colonialism and his
particular personal interest in adventure novels set in exotic places.

Zischler, Hanns, *Kafka Goes to the Movies*, trans. Susan H. Gillespie (Chicago:
University of Chicago Press, 2003). A richly illustrated study, which
traces Kafka's references to the cinema in his diaries and letters with the
help of fascinating archive material.

Index

Cambridge Introductions to...

Printed in the United States
By Bookmasters